DRUGS
The Straight Facts

LSD

DRUGS The Straight Facts

■ DRUGS
The Straight Facts

LSD

M. Foster Olive, Ph.D.

Consulting Editor

David J. Triggle

University Professor
School of Pharmacy and Pharmaceutical Sciences
State University of New York at Buffalo

CHELSEA HOUSE
PUBLISHERS

An imprint of Infobase Publishing

Drugs: The Straight Facts: LSD

Copyright © 2008 by Infobase Publishing

All rights reserved. No part of this book may be reproduced or utilized in any form or by any means, electronic or mechanical, including photocopying, record-ing, or by any information storage or retrieval systems, without permission in writing from the publisher. For information contact:

Chelsea House
An imprint of Infobase Publishing
132 West 31st Street
New York NY 10001

Library of Congress Cataloging-in-Publication Data
Olive, M. Foster.
  LSD / M. Foster Olive, David J. Triggle.
    p. cm. — (Drugs: the straight facts)
  Includes bibliographical references and index.
  ISBN-13: 978-0-7910-9709-0 (alk. paper)
  ISBN-10: 0-7910-9709-9 (alk. paper)
  1. LSD (Drug) I. Triggle, D. J. II. Title. III. Series.
  RM666.L88O45 2008
  613.8'3—dc22
                                    2008013096

Chelsea House books are available at special discounts when purchased in bulk quantities for businesses, associations, institutions, or sales promotions. Please call our Special Sales Department in New York at (212) 967-8800 or (800) 322-8755.

You can find Chelsea House on the World Wide Web at
http://www.chelseahouse.com

Text design by Terry Mallon
Cover design by Ben Peterson
Printed in the United States of America

Bang EJB 10 9 8 7 6 5 4 3 2 1

This book is printed on acid-free paper.

All links and Web addresses were checked and verified to be correct at the time of publication. Because of the dynamic nature of the Web, some addresses and links may have changed since publication and may no longer be valid.

Table of Contents

The Use and Abuse of Drugs

The issues associated with drug use and abuse in contemporary society are vexing, fraught with political agendas and ideals that often obscure information that teens need to know to have intelligent discussions about these very real problems. *Drugs: The Straight Facts* aims to provide this essential information through straightforward explanations of how an individual drug or group of drugs works in both therapeutic and non-therapeutic conditions, with historical information about the use and abuse of specific drugs, with discussion of drug policies in the United States, and with an ample list of further reading.

The series uses the word *drug* to describe psychoactive substances that are used for medicinal or nonmedicinal purposes. Included in this broad category are substances that are legal—and some that are illegal. It is worth noting that humans have used many of these substances for hundreds, if not thousands, of years. For example, traces of marijuana and cocaine have been found in Egyptian mummies; the use of peyote and Amanita fungi has long been a component of religious ceremonies worldwide; and alcohol production and consumption have been an integral part of the social and religious ceremonies of many human cultures. One can speculate about why early human societies chose to use such drugs. Perhaps anything that could provide relief from the harshness of life—anything that could make the poor conditions and fatigue associated with hard work easier to bear—was considered a welcome tonic. Life was likely to be, according to seventeenth century English philosopher Thomas Hobbes, "poor, nasty, brutish, and short." One can also speculate about modern human societies' continued use and abuse of drugs. Whatever the reasons, the consequences of sustained drug use are not insignificant—addiction, overdose, incarceration, and drug wars—and must be dealt with by an informed citizenry.

The problem that faces our society today is how to break the connection between our demand for drugs and the willingness of largely outside countries to supply this highly profitable trade. This is the same problem we have faced since narcotics and cocaine were outlawed by the Harrison Narcotic Act of 1914, and we have yet to defeat it despite current expenditures of approximately $20 billion per year on "the war on drugs." The first step in meeting any challenge is always an intelligent and informed citizenry. The purpose of this series is to educate our readers so that they can make informed decisions about issues related to drugs and drug abuse.

SUGGESTED ADDITIONAL READING

Courtwright, David T. *Forces of Habit, Drugs and the Making of the Modern World*. Cambridge, Mass.: Harvard University Press, 2001. David T. Courtwright is professor of history at the University of North Florida.

Davenport-Hines, Richard. *The Pursuit of Oblivion: A Global History of Narcotics*. New York: Norton, 2002. The author is a professional historian and a member of the Royal Historical Society.

Huxley, Aldous. *Brave New World*. New York: Harper & Row, 1932. Huxley's book, written in 1932, paints a picture of a cloned society devoted only to the pursuit of happiness.

David J. Triggle, Ph.D.
University Professor
School of Pharmacy and Pharmaceutical Sciences
State University of New York at Buffalo

1

Overview of Hallucinogens

About 5 minutes after Paul put the LSD tab on his tongue, he sat down next to his stereo and cued up his CD player to play Pink Floyd's Dark Side of the Moon. *He put on his headphones so he could turn up the music as loud as he wanted without disturbing any neighbors. While waiting for the effects of the LSD to kick in, he gazed at the artwork of the album cover, which depicted a single beam of white light striking a prism and then bursting into a rainbow of colors.*

Within a few minutes, the album cover seemed to come to life, and Paul became fascinated with the geometric patterns of the artwork. The colored lines began to take on an emotional symbolism to him, with red symbolizing anger, blue symbolizing sadness, and yellow symbolizing frustration. When the music started, the rainbow of colors turned into a musical staff and notes burst into existence with each beat Paul heard through his headphones. Paul felt as if he were diving into the sea of colors, floating in a state of awe and wonder. When the lyrics of the first song began, Paul saw each word leap from the sea of colors in huge, bold, three-dimensional letters, only to disintegrate as the next word came along to replace it. Paul began to feel uneasy about his sense of floating, with increasing feelings of anxiety about sinking below the surface of the liquid spectrum. He tried desperately to cling to the huge block letters as they sprang from the multicolored water. But each new word the singer sang caused the previous word to disappear, and Paul fell back into the ocean of colors. It seemed like an eternity between the appearance and disappearance of each word. Paul continued this rollercoaster ride of clinging to the words for safety and the uneasiness of falling back into the colored sea for about four hours, until the effects of the LSD began to slowly wear off.

A **hallucination is something that** we sense (i.e., hear, see, smell, feel, or taste) but that is not really present. Visualizing a doorway that changes into a portal to another galaxy, and seeing billions of galaxies swirling in concert as you float through this portal, or feeling as if your arms and legs have turned into tree limbs, are examples of hallucinations. Hallucinations are commonly experienced by people who suffer from mental disorders, such as schizophrenia. Many people with schizophrenia also commonly experience **auditory** hallucinations, hearing voices telling them to do things, when in fact the voices are not real but are rather a malfunction of the brain. These hallucinations are often frightening and disturbing to the person.

However, some people find certain types of hallucinations enjoyable and stimulating—and sometimes even life-changing spiritual or mystical experiences. These people may recreationally use mind-altering substances called **hallucinogens**, often called **hallucinogenic** or **psychedelic** drugs. Hallucinogens are powerful substances that can produce alterations in the senses or in such things as how body image or the passage of time are perceived. Although hallucinogens have been used for centuries in religious ceremonies by some cultures, the use of hallucinogens for recreational purposes in the United States did not become popular until the cultural revolution of the 1960s, and the use of these substances continues today.

Some hallucinogens, such as **lysergic acid diethylamide** (LSD, also known as **d-lysergic acid**), **phencyclidine** (**PCP**), or **ketamine**, are purely synthetic chemicals. Many other hallucinogens are derived from plants. Examples of these include **psilocybin** (which is found in certain types of wild mushrooms, often called **magic mushrooms**); substances derived from plants found in South America, including **dimethyltryptamine** (**DMT**) and **5-methoxy-dimethyltryptamine** (**5-MeO-DMT**);

and **mescaline**, which is derived from the peyote cactus found in the southwestern United States and northern Mexico.

GENERAL PSYCHOLOGICAL EFFECTS OF HALLUCINOGENS

Each hallucinogen has a unique chemical structure, potency, and duration of psychological effects. LSD is one the most potent hallucinogens discovered so far, with less than one

HALLUCINOGEN USE IN RELIGIOUS CEREMONIES

Although we commonly associate the rise of hallucinogen use with the "hippie" movement of the 1960s, archeological evidence suggests that hallucinogenic drugs have been used for centuries in religious or shamanic (spiritual healing) ceremonies. In this sense, hallucinogens are often referred to as entheogens, or mind-altering substances used to facilitate communication with the spiritual world, achieve spiritual enlightenment, or help in healing illnesses. Numerous cultures, including the ancient Egyptians, Greeks, Mayans, Incans, and Aztecs, have used naturally occurring hallucinogens such as the peyote cactus or hallucinogenic mushrooms. The decline of entheogens was due in part to the spread of religions such as Judaism, Christianity, and Islam, which frowned upon the use of hallucinogens. For example, the establishment of Christianity as the official religion of the Roman Empire led to the eradication of an entheogenic religious practice of ancient Greece called the Eleusinian Mysteries. Other examples include the witch hunts of the Early Modern period (about 1450–1750), where entheogen users in Western European countries such as Ireland, England, Scotland, Switzerland, and Germany were accused of devil worship, and the invasion of South America by the Spanish conquistadors, who destroyed many entheogenic religious milligram needed to produce intense psychedelic effects. A typical LSD experience, or **trip**, lasts anywhere from 8 to 12 hours. In contrast, 10 milligrams or more of psilocybin or ketamine is needed to produce any significant hallucinatory experiences, and a trip on these hallucinogens typically lasts just a few hours. Mescaline is the least potent hallucinogen, requiring about 200 milligrams to produce any psychological effects; however, the effects of mescaline typically last 12 hours

Figure 1.1 Many ancient Mexican and Native American peoples used plants such as the peyote cactus to induce hallucinations for spiritual purposes. *(© Lindsay Hebberd/ Corbis)*

practices among the continent's natives. Despite the intolerance of entheogenic practices by mainstream religions, some cultural organizations such as the Native American Church and the União do Vegetal still strive to maintain their rights to use hallucinogens as part of their religious practices.

or more. These hallucinogens are usually taken orally, and are thus absorbed through the lining of the stomach or intestines before entering the bloodstream (and ultimately the brain); this process can take 30 to 90 minutes before producing any psychological effects. A few hallucinogens, such as ketamine or 5-MeO-DMT are sometimes smoked, and chemicals carried by smoke enter the bloodstream via the lungs rapidly; this means that the onset of the drug's effects occurs within seconds.

Despite their differing chemistries and durations of action, all hallucinogens tend to produce roughly similar psychological effects. In general, hallucinogens produce a sense of slowing of the passage of time. The perception of color, touch, or sound may seem more intense. Users may feel as if their body is not their own. Shapes and objects may appear to change or "morph." The person may give increased attention to geometric patterns found in ceiling tiles, windowpanes, flooring, furniture, architecture, or artwork. Users may also experience a sense of enlightenment and **euphoria** (a feeling of extreme pleasure and well-being). Another common effect is **synesthesia**, which is the "crossing over" of certain types of perception, such as "seeing" sounds or "hearing" colors.

Hallucinogens are sometimes taken to increase one's self-awareness, and some users believe that they can communicate with God or other higher powers while under the influence of these drugs. The experience after taking a hallucinogen can vary from person to person, and is often dependent on one's personality. For example, if one has a relatively extroverted personality, he or she may feel emboldened by the drug and become very active, whereas if someone is relatively introverted and inherently timid, he or she may feel frightened by the experience. Expectations about the drug and one's previous experience with it also influence the hallucinogenic experience. If one has had a negative or frightening experience in the past after taking a hallucinogen, he or she may be more likely to have the same type of negative experience when taking it again, or even be inclined to not take the drug at all. Finally, the social setting in which the drug is taken can strongly influence the type of experience one has under the influence of a hallucinogen. Some people may prefer to be alone after taking the drug so they are less distracted by the presence of others and can concentrate more on their altered sensory perceptions, whereas other people may prefer to take the hallucinogen surrounded by friends.

Physical effects that are commonly produced by hallucinogens include dilation of the pupils, dizziness, nausea, and increases in heart rate, blood pressure, and body temperature. The intensity of these physical effects is dependent on dosage and an individual's biological makeup. For example, people with "weak" stomachs may experience nausea quite easily, whereas those with "strong" stomachs may not feel nauseous at all. The physical effects of hallucinogens are caused by the active hallucinogenic chemical itself, as well as other chemicals found within the drug. For example, magic mushrooms and peyote contain thousands of substances, many of which can contribute to the physical effects of the drug.

DANGEROUS EFFECTS OF HALLUCINOGENS

Hallucinogens are not considered to be highly addictive in the same sense as drugs like cocaine, methamphetamine, heroin, nicotine, or alcohol. People rarely become physically dependent on hallucinogens, and seldom experience **withdrawal** symptoms after stopping their use. Also, hallucinogen users rarely go on hallucinogen "binges," taking them in large amounts over a period of several days.

However, there are dangers associated with the use of hallucinogenic drugs. Sometimes users will experience a **bad trip**, characterized by frightening hallucinations and intense fear and anxiety that last for hours. People experiencing a bad trip can sometimes be calmed down by the consoling words of a friend, whereas other individuals experience such prolonged feelings of panic that they must be taken to a hospital and given tranquilizers. Bad trips are fairly unpredictable, which is one of the greatest dangers of taking hallucinogens. Often the bad trip is triggered by a frightening image, but sometimes the anxiety and fear may grasp the person without any identifiable cause. Scientists are unsure what causes bad trips, but research thus far suggests that they are a result of interactions between the drug, an individual's personality, and the environment in which the drug is taken.

Bad trips can result in **flashbacks**, or sudden recurrences of images, memories, or "reliving" of a negative experience that occurred during a previous psychedelic experience. These flashbacks can occur weeks, months, or years after the drug is used and are sometimes persistent. They are like forgotten bad memories that creep into consciousness at unpredictable times and places. Scientists are unsure precisely what causes hallucinogen-induced flashbacks, just as they are unsure why combat veterans or victims of severe trauma often experience flashbacks. Some scientists speculate that flashbacks of any kind are a result of long-lasting changes in connections between nerve cells in the brain caused by the experience. Most scientists are confident that they are not a result of the drug remaining in the body for long periods of time. Some frequent users of hallucinogens may never experience a flashback, or a flashback may occur in an individual who has taken a hallucinogen only once. Occasionally, use of hallucinogens such as LSD can result in a complete psychotic breakdown that lasts for days or weeks. This state is characterized by a loss of touch with reality and mental problems such as **delusions** (false beliefs) and **paranoia**. Although these breakdowns are rare, they tend to occur in people with pre-existing psychiatric disorders such as schizophrenia.

TRENDS IN HALLUCINOGEN USE

The popularity of hallucinogens such as LSD exploded in the 1960s and 1970s, and their use continues today, but only as a small fraction of people who use illegal drugs.[1] Males and

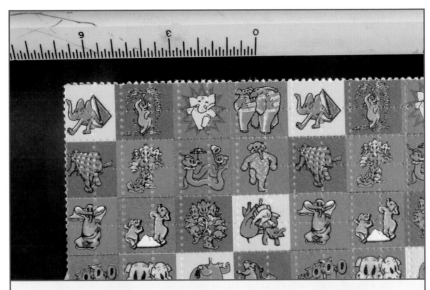

Figure 1.2   LSD is commonly seen in sheets of colorful perforated tabs that look like sheets of postage stamps. Each tab is a dose of LSD.   *(U.S. Drug Enforcement Administration)*

females use LSD in roughly equal proportions, and overall use of hallucinogens remained steady between 2001 and 2005. However, in the 1990s and early 2000s there was a dramatic spike in the number of people using a substance called 3,4-methylenedioxymethamphetamine (**MDMA**), also known as **ecstasy**. Ecstasy is chemically similar to methamphetamine and produces intense feelings of love and euphoria. It also produces enhancements in the perception of colors, sounds, and music, and for these reasons it is sometimes classified as a hallucinogen. LSD and ecstasy appear to be the most frequently used hallucinogens, according to a 2002 survey.[2]

HOW HALLUCINOGENS WORK IN THE BRAIN

In the brain, **neurons** carry electrical signals along wire-like nerve fibers called **axons**. Axons can range from less than a millimeter in length to up to several centimeters. At the end of each axon is a mushroom-shaped nerve ending called a

synaptic terminal. When the electrical signal traveling down the axon reaches the synaptic terminal, it causes chemical messengers called **neurotransmitters** to be released and secreted onto nearby neurons. This junction between a synaptic terminal and a nearby neuron is called a **synapse**. There are billions of synapses in the brain, and each neuron can have as many as 10,000 different synapses on it. After neurotransmitters are released, they diffuse away from the synaptic terminal into the synapse and encounter proteins called **receptors** on the surface of nearby neurons. Receptors are specific proteins that

SLANG TERMS FOR LSD

The most common slang term for LSD is "acid," because one of its chemical names is d-lysergic acid. Sometimes users will even shorten these terms to one letter, such as "L" or "A." However, there are a host of other slang terms for LSD, including "sugar" and "cubes" (when the drug is sold as small white crystal cubes similar in shape to sugar cubes). LSD is most often sold in perforated tabs (like a sheet of postage stamps), and so it has been given nicknames such as "blotter acid," "paper acid," "tabs," "dots," "microdots," "stamps," or "panes" (like window panes). Individual tabs, also called "hits" since they contains enough LSD to produce a vivid psychedelic experience, often have designs printed on them, such as images of comic book or cartoon characters, political symbols, or animals. Thus, some people may refer to specific LSD tabs by what is printed on them, calling them "elephants," or "strawberries." Other slang names for LSD include "animal," "barrels," "big D," "battery acid," "black star," "blue heaven," "blue moons," "blue mist," "boomers," "California sunshine," "domes," "frogs," "mind blow," "orange sunshine," "orange barrels," "snowmen," "white lightning," or "yellow sunshine." Sometimes LSD users take the drug in combination with other hallucinogens like ecstasy, which is commonly referred to as "candy flipping."

are designed to recognize specific neurotransmitters. When activated by neurotransmitters, these receptors can cause the nerve cell on which they reside to either become activated (so it passes along the electrical signal) or inhibited (so it does not pass the signal along).

Mescaline, LSD, and psilocybin produce their effects on the brain by mimicking the actions of the neurotransmitter **serotonin**. This alters how neurons communicate with each other. More specifically, these hallucinogens stimulate a sub-class of serotonin receptors called 5-HT$_2$ receptors. PCP and ketamine act by inhibiting the function of the **N-methyl-D-aspartate receptor,** which is normally stimulated by the neu-rotransmitter **glutamate**. Scientists are unsure precisely why either stimulating 5-HT$_2$ receptors or inhibiting the function of NMDA receptors results in hallucinations, but it likely has to do with how these receptors regulate the functions of neurons located in regions of the brain that control sensation, percep-tion, and cognition.

WHERE DO HALLUCINOGENS ACT IN THE BRAIN?

The brain has numerous regions that are each specialized for particular functions. So the effect of a particular drug on a person's thinking or behavior may depend partly on which region of the brain it acts upon.

Given that hallucinogens primarily affect perception, it is thought that they primarily act in regions of the brain such as the **sensory cortex** and **visual cortex.** They are also thought to act on a region of the brain involved in the perception of sound known as the auditory cortex. Finally, since hallucinogens increase one's thoughts about religion, one's purpose in life, and self-awareness, it is believed that they also act in the **frontal cortex**, where a great deal of cognition occurs. Sophisticated brain imaging techniques ("brain scans") such as functional magnetic resonance imaging (fMRI) have enabled scientists to pinpoint precisely what regions of the brain are activated by drugs such as cocaine,

SALVIA—THE NEXT NEW HALLUCINOGEN?

A recent legal battle has begun over a hallucinogenic plant called *Salvia divinorum*, which translated from Latin means "sage of the seers." Salvia (also known by nicknames such as "Sally D," "magic mint," "Ska Maria Pastora," "shepherdess' herb," and "yerba de Maria") is a member of the sage family of plants that grows in the Sierra Mazatec region of Mexico. Salvia has been cultivated and used by shamans for centuries, and its widespread use throughout Mexico is thought to have been suppressed by the Spanish Conquest. However, the use of salvia has gained popularity, particularly amongst young people, in recent years as a legal way to have a psychedelic experience.

The leaves of the salvia plant contain a psychedelic chemical called salvinorin. When eaten or smoked, the plant produces an intense dreamlike state similar to LSD or mescaline; first-time users, however, often find the salvia experience unpleasant, or obtain no psychological effects at all. If smoked, the effects of salvia peak within a few minutes or so and last for up to 20 minutes; however, if salvia is eaten, the onset of effect is more delayed and the effects last for up to an hour or two, and the psychological effects may not be as intense as if it were smoked. The leaves of the salvia plant contain other psychoactive chemicals such as salvinorins B and G; divinatorins A, D, and E; and salvincins A and B. The precise roles these chemicals play in the psychological effects of salvia are not yet known.

Some of the effects of salvia are similar to those produced by LSD. When salvia reaches its peak effects, users become easily distracted, less willing to socialize, and have altered perceptions of color and time. They may also become fascinated with geometric patterns, feel as if they are floating, experience intense feelings of spirituality and understanding, and feel as if they can communicate with higher powers. They

Figure 1.3 *Salvia divinorum.* (© Edward Kinsman / Photo Resarchers, Inc.)

may even experience full blown hallucinations and out-of-body experiences. Also, like users of LSD, salvia users rarely report any type of hangover effect and they seldom become addicted, but they do sometimes experience bad trips and flashbacks.

Salvia is currently legal in most of the United States, and is sold in some tobacco shops as well as on the Internet. However, the Drug Enforcement Agency has salvia on its "watch list" and is considering making it a controlled substance. Several states have placed their own restrictions on the salvia plant. For example, in Louisiana it is illegal to purchase or distribute salvia if it is intended for human consumption. States such as Missouri and Delaware have classified salvia as a Schedule I controlled substance, making it illegal to possess or distribute. Currently, other states such as New York and Alaska are considering similar classification. Salvia has been banned or restricted in several other countries including Australia, Belgium, Italy, and Sweden.

Table 1.1 Regions of the Brain

REGION	FUNCTION
frontal cortex	involved in planning, thinking, memory, and decision making
motor cortex	controls movement of the face, arms, and legs
sensory cortex	involved in perception of touch
visual cortex	processes sight and vision
cerebellum	controls motor coordination, balance
brainstem	controls basic bodily functions like chewing, swallowing, heart rate, and breathing
hypothalamus	controls metabolism, sleep, eating, and drinking
limbic system*	controls emotions, memory, and motivation

*Note: The limbic system is made up of several brain structures such as the **hippocampus**, **amygdala**, and **basal forebrain**.

heroin, and methamphetamine. However, because advanced brain imaging techniques are very expensive, and because hallucinogens are not considered addictive or a major public health problem, the funding for research on hallucinogens using brain imaging has not been given a high priority by the U.S. government. Brain scans are more frequently used to determine the long-term effects of chronic drug or alcohol use on the normal functioning of the brain.

2

History of LSD

I lay down and sank into a not unpleasant intoxicated-like condition ... I perceived an uninterrupted stream of fantastic pictures, extraordinary shapes with intense, kaleidoscopic play of colors. After some two hours this condition faded away.[1]

—Dr. Albert Hofmann, discoverer of LSD

THE DISCOVERY OF LSD

LSD was discovered in November 1938 by a Swiss chemist named Dr. Albert Hofmann. Hofmann was born in Baden, Switzerland, in 1906, and studied the chemistry of plants and animals at the University of Zurich. After receiving his doctorate, Hofmann became a chemist at Sandoz Laboratories (now Novartis), located in Basel, Switzerland, where he performed research on isolating medically useful derivatives of a type of fungus called **ergot** (scientific name *Claviceps purpurea*), which grows on crops such as rye and other grains that are used to make bread. Previously, scientists at Rockefeller University in New York had identified a chemical from the ergot fungus called lysergic acid, and Hofmann believed that derivatives of this chemical could have potential use in the treatment of migraines and ailments of the respiratory and circulatory systems. In one series of experiments, Hofmann mixed lysergic acid with a chemical called diethylamide to form lysergic acid diethylamine (the German name was *lyserg saeure diathylamid*, which was given the abbreviation LSD). Since Hofmann was attempting to synthesize a large number of lysergic acid derivatives, he called this one

21

Figure 2.1   Dr. Albert Hofmann.   *(© AP Images)*

LSD-25, since it was the twenty-fifth compound synthesized in his set of experiments.

Following the synthesis of LSD-25, Hofmann and his colleagues administered the substance to laboratory animals but found that it showed none of the desired effects they were looking for (i.e., increased circulation and respiration) so further research on LSD-25 was abandoned. However, in 1943,

Hofmann resumed work on his LSD derivatives. One day while attempting to make a crystallized form of LSD-25, he accidentally contaminated himself and absorbed some of the chemical through his skin on his fingertips. Soon he began to feel dizzy and restless, so he decided to go home to rest and recover. It was there Hofmann had a vivid hallucinogenic experience. ₁

Although Hofmann is often credited with discovering LSD and its hallucinogenic properties, it is likely that many people throughout Europe actually experienced similar hallucinations prior to the twentieth century. There are many reports of outbreaks of **ergotism**, or poisoning from the ergot fungus, as a result of eating bread or other products made from rye or grains contaminated with ergot, dating as far back as the Middle Ages.[2] Some of the poisonings were characterized by swelling of the hands, limbs, and feet and accompanied by severe burning pain in the arms, hands, legs, and feet, whereas in other instances of ergotism people suffered from **delirium**, hallucinations, muscle spasms, and diarrhea. It is believed that many thousands of people died from ergotism in European countries such as France, Germany, and England, and recorded history shows that such poisonings occurred as early as the tenth century A.D.

HOFMANN'S SECOND LSD EXPERIENCE—
"BICYCLE DAY"

After a five-year hiatus from his research on LSD, Albert Hofmann returned to research on the drug in April 1943 by intentionally taking 250 micrograms (one-quarter of a milligram) of LSD. Within an hour, Hofmann found himself unable to speak clearly, and asked his laboratory assistant to help him return to his home on his bicycle. As he rode home with the help of his assistant, his hallucinations and perceptual distortions worsened, and by the time he reached home he summoned his physician as well as a neighbor to bring some milk to help relieve his symptoms. Hofmann's hallucinations had become so intense and bizarre that he believed he was possessed by a demon, his neighbor was a witch, and that Albert Einstein was pursuing him with a kitchen knife. However, Hofmann's physician saw no abnormal physical symptoms other than dilated pupils, and sent him to bed to rest. After several hours, Hofmann's frightening delusions and hallucinations faded into a more pleasurable experience, with his vision filled with colorful hallucinations of geometric designs and sounds morphing into visual occurrences. Eventually

THE FIRES OF SAINT ANTHONY

Ergot poisonings, or ergotisms, are often accompanied by fiery, burning pain in the arms, hands, legs, and feet. These ergotisms were commonly blamed for mass poisonings attributable to breads and products made with ergot-contaminated ryes and grains. These poisonings became commonly known as "Saint Anthony's fire" because of the burning sensation in the limbs caused by the poisoning and also because the monks of the Order of Saint Anthony in Europe were known for their medical skills and had developed successful treatments for ergotisms, mainly by removing rye from the diet of the victim. In 1951, a mass poisoning took place in a French town called Pont-Saint Esprit, and it was immediately assumed to be a result of ergotism. Many experts, including Albert Hofmann, visited the site of the mass poisoning and took samples of the suspected bread products, testing them for the presence of ergot-derived substances. No traces of ergot were found in any of the bread samples, and many historians today argue that the other historical poisonings were not a result of ergot poisoning, but rather from poisoning from exposure to mercury (which was commonly used as a chemical to kill fungi growing on crops until it was found to have harmful effects on the body). Although both ergotism and mercury poisoning have just a few similar symptoms, a non-medically trained person can easily mistake them for one another.

Hofmann fell asleep and by the next morning his hallucinations were gone, although he reported that all of his senses appeared to still be heightened.

Hofmann retired from Sandoz Laboratories in 1971. He spent the last three decades of his life traveling, writing books, and giving lectures on LSD. Hofmann died on April 30, 2008, at the age of 102.

Figure 2.2   The ergot fungus (dark brown) growing on wheat. Symptoms of ergot poisoning include hallucinations, nausea, constriction of the blood vessels—which in severe cases can lead to gangrene in the fingers or toes.   *(© Nigel Cattlin / Visuals Unlimited)*

LSD AS AN EXPERIMENTAL PSYCHIATRIC DRUG

In the years following Hofmann's hallucinatory experience with LSD, the drug's manufacturer, Sandoz Laboratories, continued to conduct experiments in Germany on both laboratory animals and humans to assess the potential benefits of the drug in treating psychiatric disorders. Although the drug did not seem to have much of a behavioral effect on laboratory animals, Sandoz researchers were able to determine the doses at which LSD became toxic. In humans, Sandoz researchers found that LSD produced spiritual-like experiences and a deepening of self-awareness and understanding, and thus proposed use of the drug in psychotherapy. In some instances, LSD seemed to reduce the desire to drink alcohol, leading Sandoz scientists to the belief it might be of use in the treatment of alcoholism. In 1948, the drug was introduced in the United States as a potential cure for many psychiatric illnesses; soon LSD use for psychotherapy flourished and was embraced by many psychiatrists and psychologists alike (see Chapter 6 for more on this topic). During the 1950s, more than 1,000 articles about LSD were published in scientific journals, covering such topics as its use in psychotherapy to treat psychiatric illness and alcoholism to biochemical studies in laboratory animals. Some psychiatrists even began to "self-prescribe" LSD for their own use; many also taught their psychiatry students about the bizarre experiences of schizophrenic patients who had taken LSD.

One noted physician who promoted the medical use of LSD was Dr. Humphry Osmond, a psychiatrist from England who immigrated to Canada to pursue his studies on LSD. Osmond was friends with a renowned British intellectual named Aldous Huxley, who had written the futuristic novel *Brave New World*. Huxley had been experimenting with the hallucinogen mescaline (given to him by Osmond), but as the popularity of LSD grew, Huxley became interested in this drug and tried it himself numerous times. Huxley wrote hundreds of pages in his personal journal about his experiences with LSD and mescaline, which were eventually published in his books *The Doors of Perception* (1954) and *Heaven and Hell* (1956). These books described in detail the psychological and spiritual insight that Huxley achieved through the controlled use of hallucinogens. Huxley writes, "To be shaken out of the ruts of ordinary perception, to be shown for a few timeless hours the outer and inner world, not as they appear to an animal obsessed with survival or to a human being obsessed with words and notions, but as they are apprehended, directly and unconditionally, by mind at large [Huxley's term for the mind under the influence of psychedelic drugs, which he contended was more aware and perceptive than under ordinary circumstances]—this is an experience of inestimable value to everyone and especially to the intellectual."[3] Huxley's writings inspired many people to experiment with LSD and other hallucinogenic substances, but unfortunately many of these people did not adhere to the strict self-control of how much drug was taken and in what settings that Huxley did in his self-experimentation. Huxley's intent was not to "trip out" on acid in a party-like atmosphere, but to seek a higher and more enlightened mindset through the controlled used of hallucinogenic substances, similar to that used in shamanism. But readers of Huxley's writings were often too intrigued by the mind-blowing psychedelic experiences produced by LSD, rather than its ability to provide insight into the self and the spiritual world. As a consequence, the use of hallucinogens as "party" drugs predominated among the impressionable readers of Huxley's works in the middle of the twentieth century.

In 1960, Huxley was diagnosed with cancer and his health began to deteriorate. In 1963, on his deathbed and unable to speak, Huxley wrote a note to his wife requesting "100 μg LSD i.m.,"[4] which meant he wished to receive 100 micrograms of LSD via an **intramuscular** injection. She obliged, and a few hours later, Huxley passed away, on September 22, 1963.

THE BIRTH OF THE LSD SUBCULTURE

With so many scientific publications on the potential benefits of LSD, as well as the many psychiatrists who were using or prescribing it, LSD tablets eventually became available for purchase (albeit illegally) on the streets by the millions in the early 1960s. Despite media reports that LSD could cause frightening hallucinations and flashbacks, the psychedelic properties of LSD led to an explosion of its popularity among young people in the 1960s. The 1960s were a turbulent time in the United States, with many years of protest and civil unrest fueled by the civil rights movement and controversy over the Vietnam War. In addition, many of America's youth felt alienated and found satisfaction by rebelling against authority; the use of mind-altering substances such as LSD provided not only a way to rebel against authority, but for many the drug's entheogenic qualities also gave a strong reconnection with people, nature, and spirituality.

With marijuana use already prevalent among younger people, LSD became another way by which America's youth could rebel against society and authority. The hallucinogenic effects of LSD were primarily responsible for its attractiveness, but others felt that LSD offered a way to become more in touch with the spiritual world and a way to enlighten their own perspective on life, society, and their individual role in the universe.

LSD and other hallucinogens such as mescaline often promote the user to engage in a high amount of **introspection**, or self-examination and self-awareness. These practices are among the central tenets of Eastern religions such as Buddhism, which teach searching for God "within" by introspection and meditation. This is in stark contrast to the teachings of Western religions such as Judaism and Christianity, which teach the seeking of God as an external entity. As a result of these effects of LSD, the practice of Eastern religions in the United States became increasingly popular among the youth of the LSD subculture.

LSD also heavily influenced popular culture through art and music. Psychedelic art and its incorporation into advertising became extremely popular in the 1960s. LSD was known to heavily influence the lyrics and music of bands like The Beatles, The Byrds, The Grateful Dead, Jimi Hendrix, and Jefferson Airplane. Aldous Huxley's *The Doors of Perception* had such a profound influence on lead singer Jim Morrison that he named his band The Doors after the book, and Morrison's lyrics often quoted Huxley's writings. Such music was frequently referred to as **acid rock**. Songs such as "White Rabbit" by Jefferson Airplane and "Eight Miles High" by the Byrds were thought to be written about the effects of LSD.

During the 1960s, the LSD subculture also had a tremendous impact on literary works. Authors who wrote about their experiences with LSD included Alan Watts in *The Joyous Cosmology* (1962) and Ken Kesey in *One Flew Over the Cuckoo's Nest* (1962). Tom Wolfe's *The Electric Kool-Aid Acid Test* (1968) recounts the story of Ken Kesey and his band of Merry Pranksters (so named because they were enthusiastic users of marijuana, amphetamines, and LSD who tried to "turn on" people to the enlightening effects of psychedelic drugs in a fun-loving way) and who drove across the country in a psychedelic painted school bus dubbed "Furthur." On their cross-country travels, Kesey and his band of Pranksters attained numerous personal revelations through the use of LSD and other psychedelic drugs and gave LSD to anyone who was willing to try it. Following his bus trip, Kesey and his followers ended up in Palo Alto, California, where they conducted "acid tests," during which people were given LSD for free to see if it was able to expand their consciousness. The rock band The Grateful Dead frequently provided music at these "acid tests."

LSD IS MADE ILLEGAL

The explosion of the use of LSD in the 1960s was facilitated in part by Sandoz Laboratories, which allowed their patent on the drug to expire in 1963. This allowed anyone, even individual drug dealers and users, to manufacture it legally. However, because of increasing reports in the media about bad trips and flashbacks, the U.S. Congress passed the Drug Abuse Control Amendment in 1965, which outlawed the manufacture and sale of LSD and other hallucinogens except for medical use or scientific research. This law, however, did not make it illegal for an individual to possess LSD.

TIMOTHY LEARY

One of the most famous users and advocates of LSD was a man named Timothy Leary. Leary was a clinical psychologist at Harvard University who, along with his colleague Richard Alpert (later known as Ram Dass), began experimenting with LSD in the early 1960s. Leary was a strong proponent of the notion that hallucinogenic drugs were a good way to "free" one's psyche, learn more about oneself, and gain a better understanding of life and the universe. Leary also founded the Harvard Psychedelic Drug Research Program in 1960, in which he gave LSD to many graduate students and his fellow professors at Harvard, as well as some well-known artists, writers, and musicians including Jack Kerouac, Aldous Huxley, and Thelonious Monk. Leary also gave magic mushrooms to many of his colleagues under a project entitled the Harvard Psilocybin Project. However, Leary's work became increasingly controversial because of academic and government policies opposing drug use, and Leary was dismissed from Harvard in 1963. Yet Leary continued advocating the use of LSD on his own, despite frequent brushes with the law, and became the leader of the pro-psychedelic group the League for Spiritual Discovery (another famous pro-LSD group inspired by Leary was the Brotherhood of Eternal Love, which mainly operated in California[5]). Leary is credited with coining the pro-LSD phrase "Turn on, tune in, and drop out," and was often referred to as the "Galileo of Consciousness." He died in 1996.

Although this new law protected LSD use in scientific research, the Food and Drug Administration demanded that LSD researchers halt their studies and forfeit their supply of LSD. In 1966, congressional hearings were held on whether or not LSD research should be allowed to continue. Despite testimony from several noteworthy individuals, such as Robert Kennedy, emphasizing that LSD research should continue, the National Institute of Mental Health (NIMH), which had

Figure 2.3 Timothy Leary. *(© AP Images)*

funded numerous LSD projects, withdrew the majority of its funding for LSD research. In 1970, Congress passed the Controlled Substances Act, which categorized all controlled substances into one of five categories, or **schedules** (see Appendix 1). LSD was classified as a Schedule I controlled substance, which means it has no medical value and has many potential health risks. In 1971, the United Nations followed suit and made LSD illegal in the U.N. Convention on Psychotropic Substances, which most countries throughout the world eventually signed. LSD continues to be classified as a Schedule I controlled substance today in the United States.

Penalties for possession of LSD vary from state to state, ranging from fines of around $5,000 to up to 10 years imprisonment. However, possession of large quantities of LSD (i.e., upward of approximately 10,000 doses) results in much harsher penalties, including 5 to 40 years in prison and $5 million in fines.

MORE RECENT TRENDS IN LSD USE

By the 1980s, LSD use had declined sharply, likely as a result of its criminalization and public awareness of its troublesome side effects. However, a resurgence in its use occurred in the 1990s, primarily among teenagers.[6] For example, according to surveys conducted on thousands of high school students by the Monitoring the Future organization, approximately 7.2 percent of high school seniors had tried LSD at least once in their lifetime in 1986, whereas in 1997 this number had almost doubled to 13.6 percent.[7]

What were the reasons for this resurgence in the 1990s? Many sociologists and substance abuse experts believe that it was primarily due to a perception by high school students that LSD was a "safe" drug.[8] Media campaigns in the 1980s aimed at educating parents and students on the dangers of drugs had shifted their focus from LSD to newer drugs like crack cocaine. In addition, LSD remained relatively inexpensive to purchase. Another probable reason for the 1990s resurgence of LSD use was the growth in popularity of **raves**, which were large dance parties that catered to high school and college students and were held in empty warehouses or other large buildings. Raves usually integrated computerized dance music with light shows, lasers, and glow-in-the-dark bracelets and necklaces. Taking hallucinogens such as LSD became common at raves because people believed that the drugs greatly enhanced their visual and auditory experience.

However, by 2006, the Monitoring the Future surveys indicated that the percentage of high school seniors who had taken LSD at least once in their lifetime had dropped back to 3.3 percent. This decline in LSD use in the early twenty-first century is likely attributable to the rise in the popularity of ecstasy as the drug of choice among high schoolers and rave-goers. This decline in LSD use can also be credited to the success of media-based efforts such as the National Youth Anti-Drug Media Campaign, which warn against the dangers of LSD.

Despite the drop in the popularity of LSD, the drug remains illegal in most countries of the world due to the general opinion of the medical community that LSD has the potential to produce significant and unpredictable bad trips and flashbacks, and that it has no established medical use.

3

Government Testing of LSD

... Over 30 universities and institutions were involved in an "extensive testing and experimentation" program which included covert drug tests on unwitting citizens "at all social levels, high and low, native Americans and foreign." Several of these tests involved the administration of LSD to "unwitting subjects in social situations." [1]

—Senator Edward (Ted) Kennedy, 1977, at a congressional hearing on covert LSD experiments conducted by the Central Intelligence Agency

Law enforcement and government intelligence agencies have long been interested in mind-altering substances and the potential to use them during interrogation of crime suspects, captured enemy soldiers, or foreign spies. In various projects spanning several decades, agencies such as the Central Intelligence Agency (CIA) conducted studies on people in an attempt to find a **truth drug** or **truth serum**—a psychoactive substance that would cause a person being interrogated to reveal secret information that he or she would normally withhold for fear of going to jail. These secret government research programs were later revealed to the public in congressional hearings in the 1970s, such as the one quoted above.

One of the first of these programs was termed Project CHATTER, which was initiated by the U.S. Navy in 1947 to attempt to obtain information from unwilling detainees or prisoners of war without inflicting physical pain or severe psychological distress, which was internationally outlawed. Project CHATTER involved the use of the hallucinogenic drug mescaline, which had been used on inmates at a Nazi concentration camp during World War II for the same purposes. However, the navy found mescaline to be an ineffective truth serum and terminated the project six years later.

The CIA, on the other hand, had initiated its own set of research programs on finding a truth serum, involving the use of numerous substances, including stimulants like amphetamines and heavy doses of sedatives such as barbiturates or heroin. These studies were conducted under the code name Project BLUEBIRD, and were based on the notion that a person in a heavily sedated and confused state of mind might unwillingly reveal information. However, this research yielded no particularly promising results, as the experimental subjects babbled nothing but gibberish when asked questions about specific information.

PROJECT ARTICHOKE

Project BLUEBIRD changed its name to Project ARTICHOKE in 1951. At this time, the CIA was becoming increasingly aware of Albert Hofmann's experiments on himself with LSD and the powerful mind-altering effects of the drug. Working in conjunction with the military, the CIA's Project ARTICHOKE conducted mock interrogations by telling military officers not to reveal a particular piece of information, then administering them LSD and interrogating them to see if they would divulge the information. An initial series of these mock interrogations showed that officers under the influence of LSD would indeed reveal secret information, yet have no knowledge of doing so after the effects of LSD had worn off. The CIA thought that they had finally found the truth serum they had been looking for, and their Office of Scientific Intelligence detailed these findings in a 1954 memorandum entitled "Potential New Agent for Unconventional Warfare."

Further studies showed that LSD did not always produce the desired effect. Sometimes the person being interrogated would give inaccurate information due to the fact that LSD was causing the person to experience significant anxiety and panic, or to completely lose touch with reality. Though it appeared to fail as a reliable truth serum for the CIA, the agency still thought it could be used in certain situations with skilled interrogators. LSD was extremely potent and only required doses of a few micrograms to produce its mind-altering effects. In addition, LSD powder was colorless, tasteless, and had no odor, so it could be easily slipped into a person's drink or food. The CIA turned to private psychiatrists with the interest of gaining more insight into precisely how LSD could be used to break down the psychological defenses of a person and gain control of that person's mind.

PROJECT MK-ULTRA

Project ARTICHOKE eventually faded away after CIA director Allen Dulles initiated Project MK-ULTRA in April 1953. MK-ULTRA, under the direction of a chemist named Dr. Sidney Gottlieb, would become the CIA's biggest program on drug-induced mind control. One of Gottlieb's first experiments was, instead of administering LSD knowingly to a subject in a laboratory setting, to administer LSD to unwitting subjects in natural settings such as in their home or at a bar. Sometimes victims would be ordinary citizens, and other times the CIA and military would slip it into each other's drinks as pranks. As expected, the victims would begin to experience hallucinations, but often these hallucinations would turn frightening because the victim was unaware of having ingested any hallucinogenic substance. (This is an example of how one's expectations can influence whether he or she experiences a bad trip.) In one instance in November 1953, an army scientist named Dr. Frank Olson slid into a deep depression after being administered LSD without his knowledge or consent. After a few weeks Olson became psychotic and delusional. He checked himself into a

THE PRISONER EXPERIMENTS OF DR. HARRIS ISBELL

In addition to experimenting on its own personnel, the CIA also experimented with LSD on various people without their knowledge or consent.[2] One such group of subjects were patients at the Addiction Research Center in Lexington, Kentucky, who had been hospitalized for drug addiction problems. In the late 1950s, the CIA paid a research scientist named Dr. Harris Isbell to experiment with LSD on the patients at the center. In one series of experiments, the patients were given LSD daily for more than 75 consecutive days. Some of the patients became paranoid, others delusional, and most experienced tremendous and frightening hallucinations.

About this time, other experimentation with LSD by scientists on prisoners were taking place at a federal penitentiary in Atlanta, Georgia, a reformatory in Bordentown, New Jersey, and the Ionia State Hospital in Michigan. The studies conducted at these sites were of a smaller scale and generally replicated Isbell's findings in Kentucky. This experimentation on unwitting human subjects violated the Nuremberg Code on medical research ethics; this code had been established after the 1945–1949 Nuremberg Tribunals revealed thousands of human experiments had been performed by Nazi soldiers and scientists at concentration camps during World War II. At the time of Isbell's experiments, there was a growing concern by the U.S. government that communist nations like the Soviet Union and China might soon develop their own LSD mind control research programs. So, since Isbell was a private citizen who was not bound by military rules of secrecy regarding the experiments, the CIA ordered that he and other civilian scientists be closely monitored in case they might try to reveal the results of their experiments to spies from enemy nations. Despite the illegality of Isbell's experiments, he was never arrested or punished for his involvement in the LSD experiments in Lexington.

hotel in New York, and committed suicide by throwing himself out of the window and landing on the street 10 floors below. Some CIA officials were reprimanded for Olson's death, but the unwitting LSD tests were only suspended temporarily.

Under Project MK-ULTRA, Dr. Gottlieb commissioned a narcotics officer named George Hunter White to set up an elaborate scenario for giving LSD to unwitting, unconsenting citizens. This project, conducted from 1954 to 1963 under the code name Operation Midnight Climax, was secretly set up to have prostitutes pick up men in local bars, bring them back to a "brothel," and slip LSD into their drinks, all the while having their behavior closely monitored by White from behind a two-way mirror. However, this operation was later discovered by other high-ranking CIA officials who objected to the use of ordinary citizens as experimental subjects, and the experiments were halted. This research generally found that the effects of LSD were too unreliable and unpredictable to yield information from drugged subjects.

THE REVELATION OF SECRET LSD EXPERIMENTS TO THE PUBLIC

The CIA and the military conducted all these LSD experiments covertly during the peak of the Cold War in the late 1940s through the 1960s. During this period, political tensions and nuclear weapons proliferations grew between the United States and Communist countries such as the Soviet Union, China, and Cuba. The experiments were brought into the public eye in December 1974 when the *New York Times* reported that the CIA had conducted illegal experiments on U.S. citizens during the 1960s. This report prompted congressional investigations (known as the Church Committee, as it was chaired by Senator Frank Church) as well as a presidential commission (known as the Rockefeller Commission) into the activities of the CIA, the FBI, and intelligence-related agencies of the military on their search for mind-control weapons. In 1975, these congressional hearings and the Rockefeller Commission report revealed the

Figure 3.1 Frank Church, a senator from Idaho, headed the Church Committee in the mid-1970s. This committee exposed the experiments the CIA and the FBI conducted on unconsenting subjects in projects such as MK-ULTRA. *(© Bettmann/ Corbis)*

CIA and the U.S. military had indeed conducted experiments on people as part of a research program on the use of psychoactive drugs such as LSD and mescaline. These hearings and report also revealed the circumstances that led to the death of Dr. Frank Olson.

Upon the recommendations of the Church Committee, in 1976 President Gerald Ford issued the first Executive Order on Intelligence Activities, which prohibited experimentation with drugs on human subjects except with explicit consent of the person participating in the experiment. Similar orders by Presidents Jimmy Carter and Ronald Reagan expanded this Executive Order to apply to all experimentation performed on humans.

Ironically, despite all the research performed using LSD and other mind-altering substances, there was never any convincing evidence that the CIA was able to successfully force information out of anyone under the influence of LSD. However, this can never be known for certain, because in 1973, CIA Director Richard Helms ordered the destruction of most of the files and documents on Project MK-ULTRA and other LSD experiments. Remaining documents pertaining to Project MK-ULTRA that have been declassified by the military are available to the public under the Freedom of Information Act.

4

Psychological and Physiological Effects of LSD

Marianne was 19 when she tried LSD during her sophomore year at college. Her roommate, Deanna, had experimented with LSD several times and recommended it as an incredible mind-opening experience. One night, the two of them dimmed the lights, put on some techno music, and sat on the floor of their dorm room. They each took a tab of LSD from some blotter paper that Deanna had stored away in her desk. Within 30 minutes Deanna started to experience a dreamlike state, fascinated by the geometric patterns of the ceiling and watching them dance to the beat of the music. Deanna lay back on her bed and enjoyed her trip over the next two hours.

Marianne's experience was not quite as pleasant. The floor of the dorm room turned to lava, and she began to feel hot and as if she was going to get burned, so she leaped up onto her bed. When she glanced out the dorm room window, the lights coming in from outside appeared to turn red and then looked as if they were blood splattered all over the window. Marianne then felt as if the mattress of the bed had disappeared from underneath her and that she was falling into a deep black hole. This falling sensation lasted for over an hour. When she arrived at the bottom of what seemed to be a deep, dark pit, she began to try to climb out. As she clawed at the walls next to her bed, she visualized that her fingers fell off of her hands and when they hit the ground they turned to snakes. As she screamed for help she saw her words floating in the air and then disintegrate into flames. Feeling frightened and helpless, Marianne curled up into a fetal position on her bed and tried to direct her attention away from this pit she felt she was in by focusing on her dorm room wall. The wallpaper's vertical striped pattern began to resonate with the beat of the music, and she saw lyrics from the music in the form of floating words passing through the stripes. This was less frightening to her, but still she felt uncomfortable and waited for the effects of the LSD to wear off.

LSD is one of the most potent hallucinogens ever discovered. The average dose needed to produce hallucinogenic effects is roughly 50 to 200 micrograms (a microgram is one one-thousandth of a milligram, which is about the weight of a few grains of salt). LSD is most often taken orally, but it can also be absorbed through the skin. Because LSD does not directly enter the bloodstream after it is taken (as do drugs like heroin which are injected intravenously), it takes anywhere from 30 to 60 minutes for the effects of LSD to begin. Depending on a person's genetic makeup and metabolic rate, the psychedelic effects of LSD can last up to 12 hours.

PHYSICAL EFFECTS OF LSD

In addition to profound hallucinations, LSD also produces physical effects on the body, and many users of the drug report one or more of the following:

- dilated pupils

- elevated body temperature

- elevated heart rate and blood pressure

- sweating

- chills

- weakness and dizziness

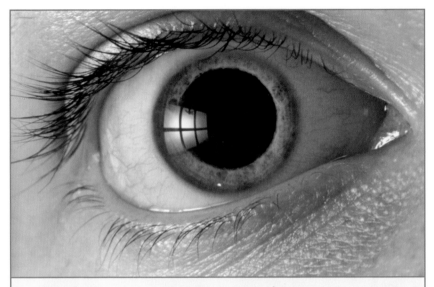

Figure 4.1   Dilated pupils, or mydriasis, is one of the physical effects of LSD, owing to the drug's stimulant effect on the body.   *(© Adam Hart-Davis / Photo Researchers, Inc.)*

- tremors

- facial flushing

- blurred vision

- nausea and loss of appetite

- insomnia

Despite its potential unpleasant physical effects, LSD is primarily taken for its hallucinogenic and psychological effects, as will be described in the following section.

PSYCHOLOGICAL EFFECTS OF LSD

LSD has numerous psychological and mind-altering effects, which are the primary motivating factors for people who take the drug. Each of the most common psychological effects of LSD is discussed below.

Hallucinations

Perhaps the most common (and desired) psychological effect of
LSD is the alteration in the perception of light, objects, sound,
smell, or touch. Many people call these hallucinations "visions"
or "visuals" and feel that they are an extremely important part
of the LSD experience. Some of the common visual and perceptual alterations that are experienced include:

- flashes of light

- objects appearing to move rapidly or change size or shape

- the geometry of objects becoming intriguing

- objects appearing to have halos of light around them

- afterimages or "trailers" appearing when objects move

- colors brightening and contrasts becoming enhanced

- images transforming into lattices, honeycombs, tunnels,
  alleys, or spirals

- the appearance of objects, animals, or people that are not
  really present, or the occurrence of vivid fantasies that are
  difficult to distinguish from reality

- "seeing" sounds, "hearing" colors

Depersonalization

A common effect of LSD is an experience called
depersonalization, which is often termed "dual existence." A
person experiencing depersonalization may feel a loss of a
sense of self or become dissociated with his or her own body.
Arms or legs may feel as if they are alien or have turned into
tree branches, even though the person still retains control
over them. Fingers and toes may appear as if they are melting
together or morphing into foreign objects such as pencils or
french fries. Depersonalization can also be described as an
"out-of-body" experience, in which the person feels as if he

SYNESTHESIA

In the 1960s, novelist William Braden experimented with LSD and mescaline and wrote about his experiences in the book *The Private Sea*. In one instance, Baden tried hallucinogens while being monitored by scientists studying the effects of LSD and mescaline on the mind. Braden took some hallucinogens while listening to a symphony by Beethoven, and as a result he began to "see" the music move about him in brilliant colors. Despite the extraordinary imagery and feelings that he experienced, Braden began to feel uneasy about his altered state of mind, and eventually became so upset by the hallucinations that he asked that his experiment be terminated and that he receive an injection of the antipsychotic drug chlorpromazine (Thorazine). It took Braden several painful days to recover from his bad trip. Braden's experience, frightening to him as it was, is an example of what is called synesthesia, or a mixing of the senses.

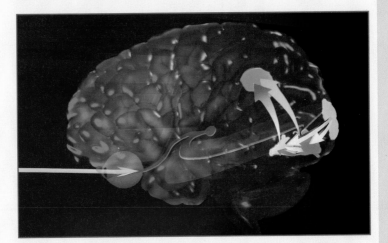

Figure 4.2 This illustration shows how the synesthesia process works. Here, visual stimulus enters through the eye and is sent to the visual cortex (yellow area). As the visual stimulus moves into the ventral stream (green and purple areas) to be interpreted, the stimulus is sent to another area (blue area); the same visual stimulus will then be simultaneously interpreted as a second sensation, such as sound.   *(© Carol Donner / Phototake)*

or she is outside of his or her own physical body. Some people experience these feelings of depersonalization as humorous or awe-inspiring, whereas others may become frightened and panic. Regardless, the experience of depersonalization is not unique to the use of psychedelic drugs. People with mental disorders such as panic disorder or other forms of extreme anxiety also can experience depersonalization, as can people enduring extreme fatigue such as that after prolonged sleep deprivation. Diseases that affect the brain such as Alzheimer's disease and multiple sclerosis can also produce symptoms of depersonalization.

Disordered Thought Patterns

Often an LSD user will experience a rapid succession of thoughts and ideas, such that their "stream" of consciousness becomes more like a raging river. Before the LSD user has time to ponder a particular idea or image, another has come along and replaced it. Although LSD users tend to concentrate largely on their hallucinatory experience, the hallucinations themselves seem to constantly morph from one distorted perception to another. For example, an LSD user who takes the drug in his or her living room may become fascinated with the fabric patterns on the furniture. Criss-cross striped fabric patterns may start to appear like complicated lattices of lines and geometric patterns. The user may spend hours watching these patterns as they change their three-dimensional configuration and become like a constantly moving visual hologram.

Altered Sense of Time and Space

LSD often distorts the perceptions of time and space. Some people feel that time slows down almost to a standstill, whereas others feel that months or years pass in span of a few minutes. Also, objects might appear much closer or farther away than they actually are (like they would in a funhouse mirror), and sometimes users have the sensation that they are looking the wrong way through a pair of binoculars.

One visual distortion that is commonly experienced by LSD users is the elongation, twisting, or sloping of hallways or tunnels. The reason this type of distortion of perception is common among LSD users is likely due to the way the drug interacts with the visual processing centers of the brain, altering the way the brain perceives depth and three-dimensional perspectives.

Memory Lapses

Although LSD users are usually quite alert and awake during their psychedelic experience, afterward they often have difficulty recalling parts of it. Much of the experience often becomes a vague memory, with the user unable to recall specific details. After the LSD trip, some users may deny the reality of his or her bizarre experience and rationalize it as being only a dream and not a real experience. Still others may have vivid recollections of specific moments of their hallucinogenic experience. Some researchers believe that memory lapses surrounding an LSD trip occur because the mind becomes so flooded with thoughts and sensory perceptions that it is unable to filter and store all the information it is processing. Others believe that the LSD experience is so mind-boggling that it is difficult to describe in words and therefore too difficult to put into details for others.

Spirituality

People who take LSD often describe their experiences as very emotional and meaningful to them, particularly if they believe they have communicated with God, Jesus Christ, or other supernatural powers. As a result, LSD experiences often result in people having changed attitudes or beliefs, a greater understanding of themselves or others, or a different way of seeing their life in the grand scheme of the universe. In some Eastern religions such as Buddhism, this type of spiritual experience is also obtained through meditation (focused, quiet thinking with the eyes closed and relaxed breathing patterns).

This commonality between the spiritual experiences of taking LSD and those of Buddhism often causes many LSD users to become more interested in the practices of such Eastern religions. LSD may also spark an interest in the user to seek out religions that promote the use of hallucinogens, such as **peyotism**, which is practiced by the Native American Church with ritualistic use of mescaline.

Emotional Changes

During an LSD experience, even minor events such as watching the sun set, seeing a shooting star, or even staring at one's own furniture or decorations can take on a tremendous emotional significance. As a result, LSD users often feel that their experience on the drug is mystical or life-changing. However, a person's emotions can also change for the worse during an LSD trip, with awe and wonder turning to anxiety and panic. For example, while an LSD trip might start off as being experienced as a pleasant and fantastic "journey," the continued hallucinations may eventually cause the person to become frightened for hours. The resulting bad trip, particularly if followed by flashbacks, may cause an enduring sense of fear, dread, and panic in the LSD user. This could result in long-lasting personality changes such as avoidance of social situations or places associated with the negative LSD experience. Bad trips and flashbacks seem to occur randomly and do not tend to occur more often in mentally fragile individuals; this is another example of the dangerous unpredictable nature of LSD.

THE PHYSIOLOGICAL BASIS OF HALLUCINATIONS

One of the principal neurotransmitters in the brain is the chemical serotonin, also called 5-hydroxytryptamine (abbreviated **5-HT**). Serotonin has many functions in the brain, including the control of mood, pleasure, hunger, sex drive, and sensation and perception. Over the years, scientists have discovered more than a dozen receptors for serotonin in the brain.

These serotonin receptors are each encoded by a separate gene located on various chromosomes.

In the mid-1950s, scientists found that hallucinogens such as LSD, psilocybin, and mescaline actually mimicked the actions of serotonin in the brain, binding to and activating specific 5-HT receptor types, namely a receptor called the type 2 5-HT receptor (abbreviated 5-HT$_2$).[1, 2, 3, 4]

So why does stimulation of 5-HT$_2$ by LSD produce hallucinations? To date, neuroscientists are still not sure, but they are beginning to piece together the puzzle. It is believed that LSD might produce hallucinations via its effects on a small region of the brain where sensory and perceptual information is processed.[5] This region, located in the brainstem, is called the **locus coeruleus** (LC) and is packed with thousands of neurons that contain the neurotransmitter **norepinephrine** (also called noradrenaline). Neurons in the LC send long axons containing norephinephrine to many regions of the brain. The LC also receives input from many areas of the brain that are involved in sensation and perception of touch, taste, smell, sight, and sound.

Scientists have discovered that the LC is packed full of 5-HT receptors, including the 5-HT$_2$ subtype, and that neurons of the LC dramatically change their activity when hallucinogens activate these receptors. The change in neuron activity modifies how norepinephrine is released in many other regions of the brain. Thus, it is likely that LSD stimulates 5-HT$_2$ receptors in the LC, which changes the ability of these neurons to respond normally to other input regarding sensation and perception. This, in turn, changes how norepinephrine is released in numerous other regions of the brain, which can then alter cognition and produce hallucinations.

Another region of the brain where LSD is thought to act to produce hallucinations and altered thinking patterns is the **cerebral cortex**. This region, which constitutes the bulk of our brain mass, is the highly wrinkled, outermost part of our brain (see Chapter 1), where thinking and planning

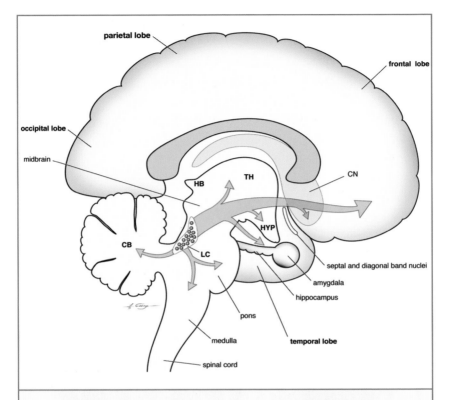

Figure 4.3 This illustration shows the normal brain pathways of norepinephrine (blue dots). Scientists believe that LSD stimulates 5-HT$_2$ receptors in the locus coeruleus (LC), changing how the receptors respond to sensory input. As a result, the norepinephrine pathways are changed, which may lead to hallucinations.
(© F. D. Giddings / Phototake)

are regulated. The cerebral cortex also processes sensory information coming from our eyes, ears, nose, mouth, and skin. As it turns out, the cerebral cortex is packed full of 5-HT$_2$ receptors, located on many neurons in this region. Scientists have found that stimulation of 5-HT$_2$ receptors in the cerebral cortex by LSD causes these neurons to release their primary neurotransmitter, glutamate.[6] In addition, the changes in the activity of neurons in the LC, which release norepinephrine onto neurons in the cerebral cortex, also produce the release of glutamate in this region. This release of glutamate likely causes disruption or hyperactivity of neurons of the cerebral cortex, resulting in the distortions in perception and logical thinking that are the trademark of hallucinogenic drugs. Similar disruptions in the activity of neurons in the cerebral cortex have been reported in people with schizophrenia.

TOLERANCE TO THE EFFECTS OF LSD

When any drug is taken repeatedly, it has the potential to produce a phenomenon called **tolerance**. Tolerance is a progressive decrease in the psychological or physiological response to a dosage of a drug when taken repeatedly over time. For example, the first time a person tries an alcoholic beverage such as beer, it may take only one or two beers to cause the individual to become intoxicated. Over time, however, with repeated drinking, tolerance develops, and more beer is eventually required to produce the same intoxicating effect. Tolerance is a result of biological adaptations in the body and brain to the continued presence of a foreign substance (alcohol, in the example above) that make it more resistant to its effects. In other words, tolerance is an attempt by the body to keep working normally despite the ingestion of an intoxicating substance. A person who takes the same dosage of LSD repeatedly may experience a progressively less intense hallucinatory experience over time, and may find that he or she needs to take higher doses of LSD to achieve the same effect. Tolerance to the effects of LSD is very rapid and profound, such that a person who takes many doses repeatedly within a few days may find that LSD may completely lose its ability to produce hallucinations, no matter how large the dose. However, a person may lose this tolerance by stopping the usage of LSD for a period of days or weeks, and therefore the next time he or she takes the drug, the first dose may again be effective in producing psychedelic effects.

IS LSD ADDICTIVE?

Can a person become addicted to LSD? Most scientists believe that, even though LSD has powerful psychological effects, it is very rare that one might actually become addicted to it. Part of this may be due to the ability of LSD to produce very rapid tolerance, but without causing withdrawal when a person stops taking it. One of the signs of addiction to any substance is that, if a person continues to take it over a long period of time and then discontinues it, he or she will experience unpleasant withdrawal symptoms such as headaches, irritability, tremors, and a depressed mood. It has been found that frequent LSD users do not experience any symptoms of withdrawal after discontinuing its use, suggesting that LSD is not physically addictive. In addition, repeated LSD use does not lead users to compulsively seek out and take the drug in an uncontrollable manner, as is seen with more addictive drugs such as heroin, cocaine, and methamphetamine.

IS LSD TOXIC TO THE BODY OR BRAIN?

Most addictive drugs are harmful to the body in some way. Chronic use of cocaine and methamphetamine increases the risk of stroke and heart attacks, long-term cigarette smoking greatly increases the risk of lung cancer, and chronic alcohol consumption causes damage to the liver. What are the risks of long-term LSD use?

Scientists still debate whether long-term use of LSD produces long-lasting or permanent damage to the brain. In a 1999 review of reports of LSD-induced psychological problems,[7] John Halpern and Harrison Pope found some evidence that LSD users have altered patterns of electrical activity in their brains, impaired visual and spatial perception, and memory deficits. These problems suggested that LSD may somehow damage the brain. However, not all studies show conclusive evidence that such psychological problems occur consistently in all LSD users, as some long-term users show no evidence of such problems.

Several laboratory studies published in late the 1960s did raise concerns about the potential toxic effects of LSD. These studies showed that incubating LSD with white blood cells in a test tube caused damage to the **chromosomes**,[8] the structures found in all living cells that contain our genetic material, DNA. Another study found that white blood cells of LSD users showed similar chromosomal damage.[9] When the news media learned of these studies, they ignited a public scare that the children of all the LSD users of the 1960s would be malformed. However, subsequent research has shown that only extremely high concentrations of LSD, which would likely far exceed the amount ingested by a normal LSD user, can produce chromosomal damage.[10] These findings, along with the fact that widespread use of LSD in the 1960s did not produce a higher than normal rate of birth defects in the children of LSD users, are commonly interpreted to mean that LSD does not cause genetic damage. However, there was one reported case that an infant of LSD-using parents was born without one of its eyes.[11] Yet it was never determined whether this birth defect was a direct result of the parents' LSD use or a randomly occurring birth defect. In general, scientists warn that, as with other types of drugs, taking psychoactive drugs of any kind during pregnancy should be avoided.

It should be noted that most LSD is largely excreted from the body within 24 hours of ingestion, and that it does not remain in the spinal fluid for weeks or months—as some urban myths have claimed.

Although these studies have not firmly established a relationship between LSD use and damage to human DNA, LSD is not considered a "safe" drug. Overdoses have been reported,[12, 13] especially when someone takes more LSD than originally intended, which can cause extreme **hyperthermia**, breathing abnormalities, and even coma. Furthermore, LSD poses a risk for more than just physical side effects. As will be discussed in the next chapter, the occurrence of flashbacks, psychosis, and a specific hallucinogen-related disorder can be psychologically harmful side effects of LSD.

5

LSD-Induced Psychological Disorders

The furniture came alive. The leather armchair morphed into a brown panther-like creature and started slowly moving toward me. As I ran into the kitchen, it followed me. I ducked into the coat closet and shut the door, but I could still hear the beast as it wandered up and down the hallway looking to devour me. I sat in the closet with my back against the door, hoping to bar the creature from entering. As I sat there I could feel sweat dripping off my brow. I kept repeating the same thought in my head over and over: "Go away. Please, go away…" I sat there in the closet for what seemed like hours, waiting for the sound of the creature's footsteps and its claws clacking on the hardwood floor to disappear. It finally did, but I couldn't leave the safe haven of the closet. I stayed there all night, wide awake and terrified of the panther returning to hunt me again.

Although LSD does not appear to be physically harmful to the body, there are many instances in which is has produced extremely unpleasant and dangerous psychological effects. LSD can produce mental breakdowns known as psychosis or psychotic reactions, bad trips, flashbacks and even a recognized psychiatric disorder known as **hallucinogen persisting perception disorder** (HPPD). Each of these will be discussed in this chapter.

PSYCHOSIS

Although many people take pleasure in the hallucinatory effects of LSD, others have reactions to the drug that are far from enjoyable. Various cases have been reported where LSD induces a type of **psychosis**,[1,2,3] which does not develop immediately after taking LSD, but appears weeks or months later and can be so long-lasting that it requires the person to be admitted to a psychiatric hospital for treatment. During a psychosis, a person loses touch with reality and becomes unable to think and communicate clearly, has inappropriate emotional responses, undergoes personality changes, and may develop paranoia or delusions. The paranoia and delusions may be extreme enough that the person becomes withdrawn or behaves in a manner that is harmful to him or herself or others. Psychotic symptoms are one of the defining characteristics of people with the severe mental disorder schizophrenia. As a result of its ability to produce psychotic symptoms, LSD is sometimes referred to as a **psychotomimetic** (a substance that mimics psychosis).

There are many factors that may contribute to whether one experiences a psychosis after taking LSD, including whether or not the person has any personal or family history of psychiatric illness, or whether the person has a history of using other psychotomimetic drugs such as cocaine, amphetamines or PCP. Some people recover from LSD-induced psychosis gradually over time, whereas others may require hospitalization and treatment with antipsychotic medications. In these people, the psychosis produced by LSD is often treated in a similar manner as psychosis in people with schizophrenia.

BAD TRIPS

A bad trip occurs when someone takes LSD and has a negative visual or emotional experience. The passage at the beginning of this chapter is a good example of a bad trip. These reactions are characterized by feelings of intense anxiety or panic, depression, confusion, paranoia and delusions, and occasionally violence toward others. Often, LSD users who experience a bad trip feel as if they have lost control over their LSD experience, believing that the hallucinations being observed are in fact real, and that they have become insane and will never return to reality. (Similarly, people with psychotic disorders such as schizophrenia also cannot distinguish between reality and their hallucinations and delusions). A bad trip may cause individuals to be unable to control their emotions—they might start crying or laughing hysterically. It may take the reassurances of a friend telling the LSD user that the hallucinations are not real and only temporary, and will go away when the LSD wears off, before the user is able to calm down. In *The Doors of Perception*, Aldous Huxley stated that hallucinogens have the potential to push one's mental state

HOW DO ANTIPSYCHOTIC MEDICATIONS WORK?

A psychosis is believed to be caused by a biochemical imbalance in the brain. This imbalance can be brought on by extremely traumatic events, drugs such as LSD, cocaine or amphetamine, or the development of mental disorders such as schizophrenia. A long-standing hypothesis is that a psychosis is a result of overstimulation of receptors for the neurotransmitter dopamine in the brain. Support for this hypothesis comes from the fact that medications that block the ability of dopamine to stimulate dopamine receptors reduce the symptoms of psychosis. These medications, which include drugs such as chlorpromazine, haloperidol, and clozapine, are known as antipsychotic medications. However, these same drugs possess the ability to block 5-HT receptors, often the 5-HT$_2$ subtype. So, by blocking the activity of 5-HT$_2$ receptors, antipsychotic medications may also block the ability of hallucinogens such as LSD to activate these receptors, thereby reducing their psychological and psychotomimetic properties.

from sane to insane. He wrote of his experience with mescaline that it was "inexpressibly wonderful…to the point almost of being terrifying. And suddenly I had an inkling of what it must feel to be mad."[4]

However, there are times when the person becomes so upset or hysterical because of the bad trip that he or she must be taken to the hospital. If further reassurances by a physician or nurse do not help calm the person down, administration of a sedative or antianxiety medication such as Valium (diazepam) may be necessary. In more severe cases, when sedatives are ineffective, antipsychotic medications may be administered. Many times, a psychiatrist is called to examine the person and verify that he or she has regained control over his or her emotions and is no longer experiencing the bad trip before the person is discharged from the hospital.

FLASHBACKS

Occasionally, several days or weeks after taking LSD, some of the bizarre or frightening perceptions experienced while under the influence of LSD can creep back into the user's consciousness unexpectedly and without warning. For example, in the passage describing a bad trip about the panther stalking the LSD user at the beginning of this chapter, the person might be walking through his or her living room days after the LSD experience and suddenly re-experience the hallucination that the armchair turned into a panther. This is called a flashback and usually involves a visual hallucination or distortion that was experienced during a previous use of LSD. Flashbacks can last anywhere from a few seconds to several hours, and often the person is unable to recognize that the hallucination he or she is re-experiencing is not real. This can be extremely frightening to the individual. Flashbacks can also be accompanied by feelings of panic, anxiety, and depression or by a tingling or numbing of the skin.

What triggers flashbacks? They usually occur a short time after the original LSD experience, and as time goes on, the

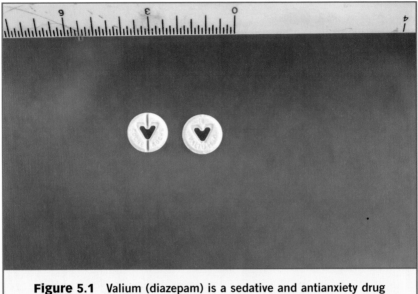

Figure 5.1 Valium (diazepam) is a sedative and antianxiety drug that can help calm people who are experiencing a bad trip. *(U.S. Drug Enforcement Administration)*

frequency with which they occur diminishes. In addition, factors such as stress, use of other drugs, dark environments, or being in the same environment in which the original LSD trip was experienced tend to be associated with the occurrence of flashbacks. Fortunately, for most LSD users, the occurrence of flashbacks fades over time.

HALLUCINOGEN PERSISTING PERCEPTION DISORDER

If LSD flashbacks persist for months or even years after taking the drug, the user would likely be diagnosed with a mental disorder called hallucinogen persisting perception disorder (HPPD).[5,6] HPPD, which was defined by the American Psychiatric Association in 1994, was previously known as posthallucinogen perception disorder. HPPD cannot be diagnosed unless hallucinogen-induced flashbacks persist beyond a few weeks or months after taking the drug. In addition, the visions or distorted perceptions cannot be a result of brain damage, infection, any other medication, medical condition, or other psychiatric disorder such as schizophrenia. Finally, to meet the diagnosis for HPPD, it is essential that the flashbacks are upsetting enough to interfere with the person's functioning in his or her job, school, or family and social life.

The flashbacks experienced in HPPD typically resemble the hallucinations experienced under the influence of the drug—flashes of light, geometric shapes, halos, afterimages, objects changing texture or shape, or a distorted sense of

FLASHBACKS AND TRAUMATIC STRESS

Users of hallucinogens are not the only people who experience flashbacks. Flashbacks are common among victims of violent crime or torture, combat veterans, and people who have witnessed horrific events such as a plane crash or serious car accident. People who experienced significant trauma may frequently re-experience the event unexpectedly, causing them great distress. Flashbacks are a common symptom of a psychiatric disorder known as post-traumatic stress disorder (PTSD). This disorder was not adequately recognized as a serious mental disorder until after the Vietnam War, when many soldiers returned to the United States and began experiencing flashbacks of the horrific events they had observed or been involved with during combat.

In the past decade there have been many cases of PTSD diagnosed in witnesses of the September 11, 2001, terrorist attacks, emergency response personnel such as firefighters and paramedics, combat veterans from the U.S. wars in Iraq and Afghanistan, and witnesses to the genocide occurring in numerous African nations. Although there is no cure for PTSD, it is treated with mild success with techniques such as cognitive-behavioral therapy, exposure therapy, and antidepressant and antianxiety medications.

space and time. The flashbacks can occur spontaneously or can be triggered by stress, anxiety, fatigue, or entering into an environment similar to the one where the drug was originally taken. The hallucinations experienced during a flashback often seem real for a short period of time, but can eventually be distinguished from reality. Symptoms of HPPD usually disappear over the course of several months, but some have reported that they can last five years or longer. The disorder can be treated with antianxiety drugs like diazepam (Valium) or antidepressants such as paroxetine (Paxil) or sertraline (Zoloft). Psychotherapy may also help patients cope with the persistent flashbacks, as well as identify potential triggers.

The earliest description of HPPD in the medical literature appeared in the mid-1950s,[7] when Dr. H.A. Cooper described eight psychiatric patients who had taken LSD for a number of weeks and subsequently developed mood swings, auditory and visual hallucinations, distortions in their sense of space and time, and changes in body image. These perceptual disturbances lasted for only one day in one of the patients (which today would not qualify for diagnosis of HPPD), but other patients in Dr. Cooper's study reported that the symptoms lasted up to three weeks, which suggested these other patients may have had HPPD.

In 1970, another group of psychiatrists reported "recurrences of trip phenomena" lasting up to three months in a group of 20 LSD users.[8] These people reported brief periods of depersonalization, disorientation, hallucinations consisting of the appearance of devil faces or color curtains, itchy skin, and feelings of anxiety, depression, and paranoia. All of these symptoms were experienced in their previous usage of LSD. Interestingly, all 20 of these users, at the time they were interviewed, were currently frequent users of marijuana. Some scientists speculate that use of other drugs such as marijuana, either during or after LSD use, may bring on the recurrence of hallucinations.

Figure 5.2   Psychotherapy can help people who have persistent flashbacks.   *(© Tom Stewart/ Corbis)*

Since HPPD has only been recognized as a mental disorder since 1994, the estimates of how prevalent the disorder is and its correlation with the number of times LSD or other hallucinogen, have been used is currently unknown, particularly since the popularity of LSD has declined significantly since its peak period of use in the 1960s.

In summary, the use of LSD has been well documented to induce a variety of psychological disorders including psychosis, bad trips, flashbacks, and HPPD. The factors that predispose individuals to develop such disorders are not well known, but have been speculated to include individual personality or genetic factors, stress and fatigue, and the use of other drugs such as marijuana or stimulants. Some individuals show symptoms of psychosis, bad trips, flashbacks, and HPPD early on in their experimentation with LSD, whereas others tend to develop these disorders after prolonged use of the drug. Psychosis, bad trips, flashbacks, and HPPD can sometimes be treated with counseling or psychotherapy, but often require more intense treatment methods such as psychiatric hospitalization and antipsychotic medications.

6

Use of LSD in Psychotherapy

LSD did not pan out as an acceptable therapeutic drug for one reason. Researchers didn't realize the explosive nature of the drug. You can't manipulate it as skillfully as you would like. It's like atomic energy—it's relatively easy to make a bomb, but much harder to safely drive an engine and make it light.[1]

—Dr. Oscar Janiger, LSD researcher

Soon after Albert Hofmann discovered the powerful mind-altering effects of LSD in 1943, the drug was introduced to the world as a potential cure for a host of mental disorders and problems, from alcoholism to schizophrenia to criminal behavior to depression. By the 1950s, LSD was a hot topic in mainstream psychiatric and psychological research, with thousands of patients being given the drug and more than 1,000 scientific and medical articles being published on the potential use of the drug in fields of psychiatry and psychotherapy.

Many researchers felt that LSD, in small doses, held great promise for helping people bring unconscious or repressed memories into consciousness in order to deal with how earlier events might be influencing their current thoughts, feelings, and behavior.[2] Psychologists and psychiatrists felt that LSD greatly increased one's level of self-awareness, which might help patients gain a greater understanding of themselves and their roles within their own relationships, families, society, and the universe as a whole. Therapy with LSD was often termed psycholytic therapy, meaning the drug had the ability to dissolve and loosen inner tensions and conflicts.[3] However, some scientists felt that, with higher doses of LSD, the experience would be so intense that it would result in a permanent personality change. From a biological point of view, many researchers felt that since the bizarre hallucinations produced by LSD were somewhat similar to the hallucinations experienced by people with schizophrenia, further study of the biochemical actions of LSD might give clues as to what biochemical abnormalities cause psychotic thoughts and behaviors in schizophrenics.

EARLY LSD RESEARCH PIONEERS

Beginning with Albert Hofmann's discovery of LSD's intense mind-altering effects in 1943, there have many psychiatrists who have pursued the use of LSD as a potential aid in psychotherapy. Here we will discuss a few of the early proponents of the use of LSD for psychiatric and psychological therapy.

Dr. Humphry Osmond

One of the first scientists to explore the potential therapeutic uses of LSD was a British psychiatrist named Dr. Humphry Osmond. Dr. Osmond had originally worked with a few colleagues in London on the psychedelic substance mescaline. They found that mescaline, which produces bizarre hallucinations similar to those found in patients with schizophrenia, had a chemical structure similar to that of adrenaline, and hypothesized that schizophrenia was possibly caused by an overproduction of adrenaline in the brain or an abnormal transformation of adrenaline into hallucinogenic chemicals.[4] (This theory is now widely accepted as being incorrect. Most theories today indicate that schizophrenia is the result of imbalances in the neurotransmitters dopamine and glutamate). In 1952, Osmond immigrated to the Canadian province of Saskatchewan where he met Dr. Abram Hoffer, another psychiatrist interested in studying the biochemical effects of hallucinogens. At first, Osmond and Hoffer found it difficult to obtain funding for their research. Their idea—that hallucinogens should be

Figure 6.1   Dr. Humphry Osmond.   *(U.S. National Library of Medicine)*

tested on people—was met with skepticism. Convinced that their ideas would revolutionize the study of mental disorders, Osmond and his colleagues began administering mescaline to themselves. After taking mescaline and proceeding to go on a walk with his wife around their neighborhood, Osmond began to experience feelings of fear and anxiety. He later wrote:

We met no people for the first few hundred yards, then we came to a window in which a child was standing and as we drew nearer its face became pig-like. I noticed two passers-by who, as they drew nearer, seemed hump-backed and twisted and their faces were covered. The

LSD AS A TREATMENT FOR ALCOHOLISM?

One evening in 1953, Osmond and Hoffer came up with the idea that since severe withdrawal from alcohol can be accompanied by hallucinations (known as delirium tremens, or DT), perhaps it shared some common biochemical mechanisms with the actions of LSD. The two then reasoned that LSD might serve as a treatment for alcoholism. They initially tested LSD on two alcoholic patients and found that one quit drinking alcohol immediately after taking LSD, and the other quit six months later. Another psychiatrist in Saskatchewan named Dr. Colin Smith tested LSD on a larger number of alcoholic patients and found that many of them curtailed their drinking habit after taking the drug.[6,7]

Smith found that LSD did not cure alcoholism by biochemically reversing or inhibiting the development of delirium tremens; rather, he noted that in some cases his patients had undergone some kind of a religious conversion after taking LSD, becoming closer to higher spiritual powers, or found a way of understanding themselves on a much deeper level, which reformed their attitudes toward drinking alcohol. Additional studies, from this Canadian province and beyond, would soon demonstrate additional successful treatments of alcoholics with LSD.

By the mid-1960s, however, many reports on the dangers of LSD, including violent behavior and flashbacks, flooded the media and soon use of LSD in any medical setting was criminalized (see Chapter 2). Despite its illegality, there are still some scientists today who firmly believe that LSD is an effective agent for treating alcoholism and that research on this topic should be decriminalized.[8]

wide spaces of the streets were dangerous, the houses threatening, and the sun burned me.[5]

When the news of LSD's hallucinogenic properties reached Osmond and his colleagues in 1953, they were intrigued and switched to the drug, which was much more readily available than mescaline, and required much less of the drug to produce its effects. Osmond was one of the first to propose that LSD might be useful in the treatment of alcoholism.

Dr. Stanislav Grof

Another early pioneer of LSD research was a European psychiatrist named Dr. Stanislav Grof, who used LSD as a tool in psychotherapy first at the Psychiatric Research Institute in Prague (in today's Czech Republic) and later in the United States and Johns Hopkins University. Grof conducted more than 4,000 psychotherapy sessions involving the use of LSD by his patients, and wrote a very influential book called *LSD Psychotherapy.* Though a strong proponent of the use of LSD in psychotherapy, Grof (as well as other LSD researchers, including Humphry Osmond) realized that LSD was just another tool in the psychiatrist's toolbox. Grof believed that the successful use of the drug in psychotherapy depended highly upon the nature of the patient, the psychiatrist administering the drug, the purpose for which LSD in therapy was intended, and the circumstances and environment in which the drug was used.[9] Grof also noted that although many of the dangerous side effects and unfortunate events that have occurred after someone has taken LSD get blamed on the drug itself, and most people often fail to see the other contributing factors that are to blame.

Dr. Oscar Janiger

Psychiatrist Dr. Oscar Janiger conducted numerous experiments on LSD between 1954 and 1962 in the Los Angeles area, especially in people with no history of psychiatric illness.

Figure 6.2 Dr. Stanislav Grof. *(© Getty Images)*

Janiger administered LSD to approximately 900 subjects as part of an experiment to further explore the nature of the LSD experience. Soon after the effects of LSD wore off, Janiger had his subjects write personal narratives of their experiences. Then, a month later, Janiger asked his subjects to complete questionnaires about their experience with LSD. However, after concerns over the possible adverse consequences of LSD use arose in the mid-1960s, people wondered whether LSD that had been given for psychiatric purposes also had negative long-term effects. So, an organization called the Multidisciplinary Association for Psychedelic Studies (MAPS) funded a follow-up study in the 1990s on the well-being of 46 of Janiger's patients decades after they had been given LSD. Only Janiger patients were examined in this follow-up study because he carefully administered the same dose of LSD to each subject (2 micrograms of LSD per kilogram of body weight), and all of his subjects had no other history of psychiatric illness. The MAPS study found that most of Janiger's patients had few bad side effects of the drug, and most reported that overall their experience with LSD was generally positive.[10] There was one case, however, of someone experiencing flashbacks that lasted up to one year, suggesting the development of HPPD.

In summary, the use of LSD in psychotherapy over the years has produced mixed outcomes, with some patients and doctors affirming its usefulness in increasing self-awareness, resolving inner conflicts, breaking down psychological barriers, inducing positive personality and attitude changes, and even curing some individuals of alcoholism. However, other patients, as well as most psychiatrists, feel that the LSD experience is too unpredictable to be used successfully in psychotherapy, and that the risks of negative, long-term consequences such as negative personality changes, flashbacks, HPPD, and mood disorders such as depression strongly outweigh any potential benefit. LSD is classified as a Schedule I controlled substance. It is viewed by the DEA as having no medical value. It is illegal to administer LSD during psychotherapy or any other medical setting without strict government regulations.

Yet there are still scientists today studying the effects of LSD, hoping to understand how the brain responds and adapts to certain types of experiences, which may lead to a better understanding of what goes wrong in the brain during certain mental disorders such as schizophrenia and depression. For example, Dr. Charles D. Nichols, a professor of pharmacology at the Louisiana State University Health Sciences Center in the School of Medicine at New Orleans, has shown in laboratory rats that LSD alters the expression of genes that regulate the formation of synapses, and that LSD may actually cause microscopic structural changes within the brain.[11,12] Dr. Nichols and other scientists continue their research today on precisely how LSD and other hallucinogens change the brain's inner workings.

7

Comparison of LSD to Other Hallucinogens

The feeling of doing DMT is as though one had been struck by **noetic** *lightning. The ordinary world is almost instantaneously replaced, not only with a hallucination, but a hallucination whose alien character is its utter alienness. Nothing in this world can prepare one for the impressions that fill your mind when you enter the DMT sensorium.[1]*

—Terence McKenna, writer, philosopher,
and user of hallucinogens

Humans have used mind-altering substances for thousands of years, and the discovery of LSD by Dr. Albert Hofmann is considered by most scientists to be the start of the modern era of psychedelic drugs. However, there are dozens of other hallucinogens that are used by people today, and this chapter will discuss several of them and how they compare with LSD.

MESCALINE AND PEYOTE

Mescaline is the primary psychoactive ingredient in the peyote cactus (scientific name *Lophophora williamsii*) that grows in certain areas of Mexico and the southwestern United States To ingest mescaline, a person cuts small buttons (approximately one inch in diameter) off the peyote cactus, dries them, and eats anywhere from 4 to 12 buttons in order to obtain the necessary 200 to 400 milligrams of mescaline required to produce psychedelic effects.

Figure 7.1 The peyote cactus (*Lophophora williamsii*) has historically been used by Native American and Mexican peoples to heighten religious experiences. *(© John Trager / Visuals Unlimited)*

Several hours after it is ingested, mescaline produces many effects that are similar to LSD, including visual and perceptual hallucinations, distortion in the sense of time and space, synesthesia, and spiritual or mystical experiences. The effects of mescaline are longer acting than those of LSD, lasting up to 24 hours. In addition, consumption of peyote buttons often causes vomiting and nausea, which some view as purging the body of toxins so that one can be clean in their search for communication with the divine. As with LSD, mescaline can also cause bad trips, flashbacks, and HPPD, although much less frequently.

Peyote buttons are typically taken by Native Americans in religious rituals. In the United States, these rituals are performed routinely (often once weekly) by members of an organization called the Native American Church. The purpose of these rituals is to cleanse oneself of impurities and evil spirits, to cure physical ills, and to communicate with supreme beings and obtain spiritual enlightenment. These rituals are typically led by shamans, or medicine men, who use peyote for its perceived healing powers. Both peyote and mescaline are classified as Schedule I controlled substances by the DEA, and are therefore illegal to possess. However, to preserve the cultural rights of Native Americans, special laws have been enacted to exempt members of the Native American Church from prosecution for harvesting, possessing, and using peyote or mescaline.

PSILOCYBIN AND PSILOCIN

There are many species of mushrooms that grow in the wild that, if eaten, produce a vivid psychedelic experience. (However, it bears mentioning that there are an equal if not greater number of wild mushrooms that if eaten are poisonous and can cause death!) These so-called magic mushrooms belong to the genera *Psilocybe*, *Panaeolus*, and *Copelandia*. These mushrooms contain significant amounts of a chemical called psilocybin, which itself is not a potent hallucinogen but is metabolized by the body into a potent hallucinogenic chemical called **psilocin**. Approximately 1 to 5 grams of mushrooms, depending on the particular species, are needed to yield a psychedelic dose of psilocin of 10 to 20 milligrams.

Approximately 30 to 60 minutes after magic mushrooms are ingested, the hallucinogenic effects of psilocin begin to take effect. The effects are similar to those produced by LSD, including visual hallucinations, intensification of perceptions, synesthesia, quickly changing emotions, and feelings of enlightenment or spirituality. The mushroom experience typically lasts three to six hours, which is often followed by a period of several hours where it is difficult to sleep and perception remains slightly distorted or "not real." Some mushroom users can experience anxiety, paranoia, and confusion, which can lead to a bad trip, but flashbacks and HPPD are less common after

Figure 7.2 Liberty cap mushrooms (*Psilocybe semilanceata*) contain psilocybin, and are one of the many hallucinogenic mushroom species. (*© Martin Bond / Photo Researchers, Inc.*)

using mushrooms than after LSD. The reasons why flashbacks and HPPD are more common among LSD users than users of mushrooms are currently unknown, but may be related to the longer duration of action and the much higher potency of LSD as compared to psilocybin. As with mescaline and peyote, some mushroom users experience nausea and vomiting. Psilocybin and psilocin are classified as Schedule I controlled substances and are thus illegal to possess or distribute.

MDMA (ECSTASY)

MDMA is an acronym for 3,4-methylenedioxymethamphetamine, more commonly known as ecstasy. MDMA most frequently comes in the form of a tablet containing 75 to 150 milligrams of the substance. Approximately 30 minutes after being ingested, MDMA produces strong feelings of love and empathy for others as well as euphoria and a robust sense of well-being. MDMA also intensifies the perception of light and sound and can produce mild hallucinations such as blurred objects, afterimages, or "trailers." However, the hallucinations produced by MDMA are less intense and less frequently experienced than those experienced after taking LSD. The effects of MDMA last approximately three to six hours.

When the effects of MDMA wear off, many people experience a **crash**, or feelings of depression sometimes accompanied by anxiety that can last for hours or days. This crash can cause users to seek out the drug again, which can ultimately lead to tolerance and addiction. Other side effects of MDMA are hyperthermia, dehydration, jaw-clenching, nausea, vomiting, and dizziness. There is some evidence that MDMA causes the degeneration of serotonin nerve terminals in the brain. As with other hallucinogens, MDMA is classified as a Schedule I controlled substance and is therefore illegal to manufacture, distribute, or possess.

2,5-DIMETHOXY-4-METHYLAMPHETAMINE (DOM)

DOM is a potent and synthetic psychedelic drug which a chemical structure similar to that of MDMA. DOM produces psychedelic effects that are very similar to those of LSD. Approximately 3 to 10 milligrams are needed to produce hallucinatory effects, which last much longer than those produced by LSD (14 to 20 hours versus 8 to 12 for LSD). During the 1960s, DOM was nicknamed STP (for serenity, tranquility, and peace). DOM comes in powder or tablet form and is usually orally ingested. Use of DOM today is rather uncommon, but the substance is still classified as a Schedule I controlled substance.

DIMETHYLTRYPTAMINE (DMT)

DMT is a hallucinogen that is commonly smoked and is sometimes taken orally. It produces intense visual hallucinations.

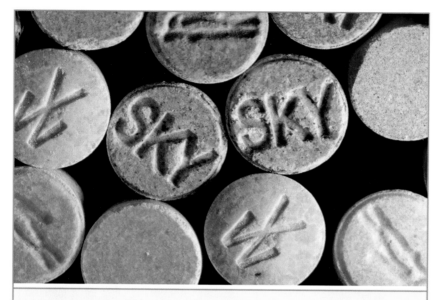

Figure 7.3 MDMA, or ecstasy, pills. *(U.S. Drug Enforcement Administration)*

Approximately 15 to 60 milligrams of DMT is needed to produce its effects when smoked, and greater than 350 milligrams is needed if taken orally. If DMT is taken orally, however, it must be taken together with a type of drug called a **monoamine oxidase inhibitor** (MAOI), which prevents the metabolic breakdown of DMT before it reaches the brain. DMT is present in many types of plants found in South America and is used in a psychedelic drink called ayahuasca.

When DMT is smoked, the effects begin in less than a minute and are extremely intense. Many users report the experience of being transported instantaneously to an alien world and interacting with alien beings. Because the onset of the hallucinatory effects of DMT is so rapid and intense, they often take the first-time user by surprise, which leads to uncomfortable feelings about their experience. Unlike LSD, however, the effects of DMT last less than one hour, giving it the nickname "businessman's trip." However, many people experience confusion or disturbing thoughts for days after taking DMT, and flashbacks and HPPD can occur. One noted person who used DMT was a writer and philosopher named Terence McKenna, whose theories about physics and the nature of the universe were deeply inspired by his hallucinogenic experiences. DMT is classified as a Schedule I controlled substance.

5-METHOXY-DIMETHYLTRYPTAMINE (5-MEO-DMT)

Similar to DMT, 5-MeO-DMT is a naturally occurring chemical found in certain types of South American plants. It has been used in snuffs and drinks for centuries. The chemical was later synthesized as a crystalline powder that can be snorted, smoked, or taken orally at doses of 2 to 15 milligrams. 5-MeO-DMT is very closely related chemically to DMT. When smoked, its effects can be felt in less than a minute. The psychedelic effects of 5-MeO-DMT are short-lived (lasting less than an hour when smoked) and include sudden and intense "visions" and changes in perspective of the universe, whereas visual hallucinations and perceptual distortions common to LSD are experienced less frequently. Snorting 5-MeO-DMT produces a slower onset of effects that last from one to three hours. Side effects include feelings of anxiety, difficulty concentrating, insomnia, and occasionally flashbacks and HPPD. Unlike DMT and LSD, 5-MeO-DMT is currently not classified under any schedule by the DEA.

5-METHOXY-DIISOPROPYLTRYPTAMINE
(5-MEO-DIPT)

5-MeO-DIPT, which is also called "foxy" or "foxy methoxy," was developed by a California professor and well-known psychedelic drug user and proponent named Alexander Shulgin around 1980. It remained relatively unknown until it started being produced in the 1990s as a chemical agent for studying hallucinogens in humans and animals. The drug usually comes in a white powdered form, and doses in the range of 5 to 30 milligrams taken orally produce extreme sensations of pleasure and exhilaration in some users, whereas in others it produces quite negative reactions such as nausea and diarrhea. The onset of the effects of 5-MeO-DIPT typically occurs in less than an hour. The drug also produces intensification of the sense of touch, visual hallucinations, and for some users an unusual erotic feeling. Occasionally, 5-MeO-DIPT can produce feelings of anxiety and muscle tension. The effects of 5-MeO-DIPT last from four to eight hours. Chemically, 5-MeO-DIPT is closely related to DMT, 5-MeO-DMT and psilocybin. The drug is currently classified as a Schedule I controlled substance.

2,5-DIMETHOXYPROPYLTHIOPHENETHYLAMINE (2C-T-7)

2C-T-7, commonly referred to as T7 or Blue Mystic, is a synthetic drug that was also developed around 1980 by Alexander Shulgin. At doses between 10 and 50 milligrams, 2C-T-7 produces colorful visual hallucinations similar to those produced by LSD. However, its chemical structure is more similar to that of mescaline. After being taken orally or snorted, 2C-T-7 can take over an hour to produce hallucinations, which last anywhere from 8 to 15 hours. As with LSD, 2C-T-7 can produce altered mood (either positively or negatively). However, at higher doses, this drug can produce some unpleasant depersonalization effects as well as panic and anxiety and loss of memory. In rare instances, 2C-T-7 can cause the user to become violent. More frequent undesirable side effects include nausea, vomiting, and dizziness. There was a surge in the popularity of this drug between 1999 and 2001 when it could be obtained via the Internet. Since that time, however, it has been classified as a Schedule I controlled substance.

4-BROMO-2,5-DIMETHOXYPHENETHYLAMINE (2C-B)

2C-B, commonly referred to as Nexus, bees, or Venus, is a synthetic psychedelic substance originally synthesized by

Alexander Shulgin that produces intense visual hallucinations. 2C-B is less likely to produce bad trips than LSD. It is taken in pill or powder form at doses of 5 to 50 milligrams, and its chemical structure is similar to that of mescaline. 2C-B takes effect approximately one hour after it is ingested, and its psychedelic effects last four to eight hours. Common side effects include upset stomach and diarrhea, as well as potential bad trips and feelings of anxiety and panic. 2C-B was originally sold to users as a legal substitute for MDMA, but in 1995 it was outlawed by the DEA as a Schedule I controlled substance.

SALVINORIN

Salvinorin is an extract of the plant *Salvia divinorum*, which grows in areas of southern Mexico. The plant is revered for its psychedelic properties and is often referred to as "la pastora" (the shepherdess), "diviner's mint," "diviner's sage," or simply "salvia." The leaves of the plant (approximately 200 to 500 milligrams for a dry leaf) are usually smoked or chewed. The main psychoactive ingredient of the salvia plant is salvinorin (which has two different forms, referred to as salvinorin A and salvinorin B), which is chemically unrelated to any other hallucinogenic substance, and does not directly interact with receptors for serotonin. Rather, it interacts with a class of receptors called kappa **opioid receptors**. When smoked, salvinorin produces psychedelic effects within one minute, which then dissipate within an hour. At higher doses, salvinorin produces many LSD-like effects, including alterations in the perception of time, vivid visual hallucinations, and the delusion that one has traveled to alien civilizations. Some people find the effects of salvinorin to be overwhelming, unpleasant, and frightening. Bad trips, flashbacks, and HPPD can be produced by salvinorin. The salvia plant is currently unscheduled in the United States, meaning it is legal to possess and sell. However, the DEA has salvia on its "watch list" and is considering making it a controlled substance.

KETAMINE, PHENCYCLIDINE (PCP), AND DEXTROMETHORPHAN

Ketamine, often referred to as "special K," is an **anesthetic** agent that is primarily used for veterinary purposes. However, ketamine is sometimes used recreationally by injecting it into a muscle or drying the liquid to form a powder residue,

ALEXANDER SHULGIN

Alexander Shulgin was born in 1925 in Berkeley, California, and in 1954 he earned a Ph.D. in biochemistry from the University of California at Berkeley. Shulgin is credited with popularizing MDMA in the late 1970s and early 1980s for its possible psychotherapeutic uses. In 1991 he and his wife Ann Shulgin authored the popular psychedelic drug book *Phenethylamines I Have Known and Loved* (commonly referred to as PiHKAL). In this book, Shulgin describes his discovery, synthesis, and self-testing of over 230 psychoactive compounds, including 2C-B and some tryptamine-related drugs such as DMT.

Shulgin's interest in psychedelic drugs was initially spurred by his experimentation with mescaline in the 1950s. After obtaining his Ph.D., Shulgin worked for various chemical companies, including Dow Chemical Company, where he discovered Zectran, the first biodegradable pesticide. In 1965, he left Dow to pursue his own research interests and eventually set up a small chemical laboratory in his own house, where he synthesized and tested on himself numerous psychedelic chemicals. Shulgin also formed a relationship with the local DEA office and began holding educational seminars for DEA agents, supplying the DEA with samples of various compounds he had created, and occasionally serving as an expert witness in court. For his services, the DEA granted Shulgin a special license for synthesizing and testing Schedule I controlled substances, which are normally illegal to possess.

In addition to testing psychedelic substances on himself, Shulgin recruited a small group of his friends on whom he which can then be snorted or dissolved for intravenous injection. Within 5 to 15 minutes of being ingested, lower doses of ketamine produce a dream-like state, relaxation, and mild and pleasurable visual hallucinations (often called "K land"), whereas higher doses can cause immobility, nausea, increased heart rate, and depersonalization experiences that are so

Figure 7.4 Alexander Shulgin. *(© Scott Houston/Sygma/ Corbis)*

regularly tested his creations. They even developed the Shulgin Rating Scale, which was a systematic way of ranking the psychedelic effects of the various drugs. However, in 1994, several years after the publication of his book, the DEA raided his home laboratory and found problems with his record keeping on substances he had created. The DEA requested that Shulgin forfeit his Schedule I license and he was fined $25,000 for possession of anonymous chemical samples sent to him for testing. Shulgin was forced to shut down his self-testing program. He currently resides in Lafayette, California.

intense they produce extreme anxiety (often called a "K hole"). The effects of ketamine can last anywhere from 30 minutes to two hours, and repeated ketamine use can lead to addiction. Because of the depersonalization or "dissociative" effects of ketamine, it is often referred to as a **dissociative anesthetic**. Because of its medical usefulness as an anesthetic, ketamine is classified as a Schedule III controlled substance.

PCP is also a dissociative anesthetic, but its medical use has largely been discontinued because of its severe hallucinatory and delusional side effects. PCP is often referred to on the street as "angel dust," "ozone," or "rocket fuel." PCP is a white crystalline powder that can be snorted, smoked, or taken orally. At low to moderate doses (3 to 10 milligrams), many of the effects of PCP are similar to those of LSD, including hallucinations, confusion, loss of coordination, increased heart rate and hyperthermia. However, PCP users tend to be much more active and driven by their hallucinations than LSD users, and often act combative, violent, or suicidal. High doses of PCP (greater than 10 milligrams) can cause psychotic episodes including delusions and paranoia, seizures, coma, and death. PCP has a high potential for producing addiction, and people who repeatedly abuse PCP can experience memory loss and difficulties with speech and concentration. PCP is currently classified as a Schedule II controlled substance.

Dextromethorphan, often called **DXM** for short, is a common ingredient in over-the-counter cough medicines. Because products containing DXM are sold in pharmacies and supermarkets, accessibility to DXM is quite easy. Since the start of the twenty-first century there has been an increase in the number of people, particularly high school and college students, who take cough suppressants in very large doses in order to experience the psychedelic effects of DXM. Low doses (100 to 400 milligrams) of DXM produce intoxicating effects similar to those of alcohol, with a slight dream-like experience. At higher doses (500 to 1,500 milligrams), DXM may produce vivid hallucinations that are sometimes frightening,

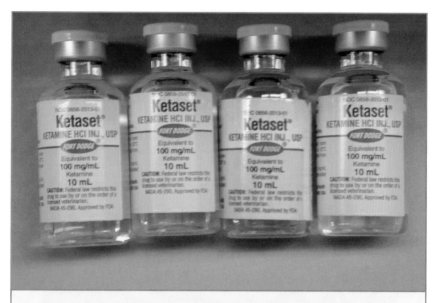

Figure 7.5 Ketamine is a dissociative anesthetic; the blocking of signals between the conscious mind and the senses can induce a dream-like state and hallucinations.   *(U.S. Drug Enforcement Administration)*

accompanied by motor incoordination, confusion, and feelings of depersonalization. Vomiting, diarrhea, and skin itching may also occur after ingestion of high amounts of other ingredients contained within the cough medicine. The effects of DXM typically last four to six hours.

Although ketamine, PCP, and DXM produce effects similar to those produced by LSD, they are chemically unrelated to the other hallucinogens previously discussed. In addition, they do not directly interact with serotonin receptors in the brain. Rather, they exert their effects by blocking a specific type of receptor for the neurotransmitter glutamate, called the N-methyl-D-aspartate (NMDA) receptor. Alcohol also inhibits the function of this receptor, and deficits in the activity of this receptor have been linked to schizophrenia.

In summary, there are a vast number of hallucinatory substances that have been, and continue to be, used by humans

Table 7.1 Comparison of pharmacological properties of various hallucinogens

	AVERAGE DOSE	DURATION OF EFFECTS
LSD	0.05-0.2 mg	8-12 hours
Mescaline	200-400 mg	12-24 hours
Psilocybin/Psilocin	10-20 mg	3-6 hours
MDMA	75-150 mg	3-6 hours
DOM	3-10 mg	14-20 hours
DMT	15-60 mg	<1 hours
5-MeO-DMT	2-15 mg	5 minutes to 3 hours
5-MeO-DIPT	5-30 mg	4-8 hour
2C-T-7	10-50 mg	8-15 hours
2C-B	5-50 mg	4-8 hours
Salvinorin	200-500 mg	15-60 minutes
Ketamine	30-300 mg	0.5-2 hours
Phencyclidine (PCP)	3-10 mg	4-6 hours
Dextromethorphan (DXM)	100-1,500 mg	4-8 hours

for their psychedelic properties. LSD is by far one of the most potent and popular. The majority of psychedelic drugs interact with the brain's serotonin system, although there are a few that interact with receptors for the neurotransmitter glutamate or kappa opioid receptors.

Most psychedelic drugs are unpredictable in whether they will produce a positive, pleasurable experience for the user or a negative, frightening experience. The type of experience depends on many factors, including the individual's personality, genetic makeup, past experiences with or without hallucinogens or other mind-altering chemicals, and the environmental context in which the drug is taken. All hallucinogens present the danger of overdose, bad trips, and flashbacks, and can potentially result in HPPD. However, it is currently impossible to predict who will have a positive experience with a hallucinogen and who will have a frightening negative experience that may have psychological consequences that will last for days, weeks, months, or years. It is this unpredictable nature of hallucinogens, particularly LSD, which makes these substances so dangerous.

Appendix 1

DRUG ENFORCEMENT ADMINISTRATION CLASSIFICATION OF CONTROLLED SUBSTANCES

In 1970, the U.S. government passed the Controlled Substances Act, which classified all drugs into one of five categories, or "schedules." In effect, this law classified drugs and other substances according to how medically useful, safe, and potentially addictive they are. These schedules are defined as follows:

Schedule I—The drug has (1) a high potential for abuse, (2) no currently accepted medical use in the United States, and (3) a lack of accepted safety. Peyote and mescaline are classified as a Schedule I substance, as are marijuana, heroin, ecstasy, psilocybin, LSD, DMT, and Foxy.

Schedule II —(1) The drug has a high potential for abuse, (2) the drug has a currently accepted medical use in the United States or a currently accepted medical use with severe restrictions, and (3) abuse of the drug may lead to severe psychological or physical dependence. Cocaine, morphine, methamphetamine, and d-amphetamine are examples of Schedule II substances.

Schedule III —(1) The drug has less potential for abuse than the drugs in schedules I and II, (2) the drug has a currently accepted medical use in treatment in the United States, and (3) abuse of the drug may lead to moderate or low physical dependence or high psychological dependence. Anabolic "body-building" steroids, ketamine, and many barbiturates are examples of Schedule III substances.

Schedule IV—(1) The drug has a low potential for abuse relative to the drugs in Schedule III, (2) the drug has a currently accepted medical use in treatment in the United States, and (3) abuse of the drug may lead to limited physical dependence or psychological dependence relative to the drugs or other substances in Schedule III. Antianxiety drugs such as Valium and Xanax, as well as prescription sleeping pills such as Ambien, Lunesta, Halcion, and Dalmane are examples of Schedule IV substances.

Schedule V—(1) The drug has a low potential for abuse relative to the drugs or other substances in Schedule IV, (2) the drug has a currently accepted medical use in treatment in the United States, and (3) abuse of the drug may lead to limited physical dependence or psychological dependence relative to the drugs or other substances in Schedule IV. Certain narcotic-containing prescription cough medicines such as Motofen, Lomotil, and Kapectolin PG are classified as Schedule V substances.

Notes

Chapter 1

1. U.S. Government Printing Office (2006). National Survey on Drug Use and Health. Substance Abuse and Mental Health Services Administration, Office of Applied Studies, Washington, D.C.
2. U.S. Government Printing Office (2002). National Survey on Drug Use and Health. Substance Abuse and Mental Health Services Administration, Office of Applied Studies, Washington, D.C.

Chapter 2

1. Hofmann, Albert. *LSD: My Problem Child.* New York: McGraw Hill, 1980.
2. Schiff, Paul L. "Ergot and its alkaloids." *American Journal of Pharmaceutical Education* 70, 5 (2006): 98.
3. Huxley, Aldous. *The Doors of Perception and Heaven and Hell.* New York: Harper Perennial Modern Classics, 2004.
4. Huxley, Laura Archley. *This Timeless Moment.* Berkeley, CA: Celestial Arts, 2000.
5. Tendler, Stewart and May, David. *The Brotherhood of Eternal Love: From Flower Power to Hippie Mafia. The Story of LSD Counterculture.* New York: Cyan Books, 2007.
6. Schwartz, R.H. "LSD. Its rise, fall and renewed popularity among high school students." *Pediatric Clinics of North America* 42 (1995): 403–413.
7. Johnston, L. D., O'Malley, P. M., Bachman, J. G., and Schulenberg, J. E. Monitoring the Future national survey results on drug use, 1975–2006.

Volume I: Secondary school students (NIH Publication No. 07-6205). Bethesda, MD: National Institute on Drug Abuse (2007): 699.

8. Hunt, D., 1997. "Rise of Hallucinogen Use." Research Brief: Publication NCJ 166607; National Institute of Justice, 1–12.

Chapter 3

1. Opening Remarks by Senator Ted Kennedy during the August 3, 1977, meeting of the U.S. Senate Select Committee On Intelligence, and Subcommittee On Health And Scientific Research of the Committee On Human Resources.
2. Lee, M.A. and Shlain, B. *Acid Dreams—The Complete Social History of LSD: The CIA, the Sixties, and Beyond.* New York: Grove Press, 1992, 24–25.

Chapter 4

1. Glennon, R.A., Titeler, M., McKenney, J.D. "Evidence for 5-HT_2 involvement in the mechanism of action of hallucinogenic agents." *Life Sciences* 35 (1984): 2502–2511.
2. Titeler, M., Lyon, R.A., and Glennon, R.A. "Radioligand binding evidence implicates the 5-HT_2 receptor as a site of action for LSD and phenylisopropylamine hallucinogens." *Psychopharmacology* 94 (1988): 213–216.
3. Fantegrossi, W.E, Murnane, K.S., and Reissig, C.J. "The behavioral pharmacology of hallucinogens." *Biochemical Pharmacology* 75 (2008): 17–33.

Notes

4. Nichols, D.E. "Hallucinogens." *Pharmacology and Therapeutics* 101 (2004): 131–181.

5. Aghajanian, G.K. "Mescaline and LSD facilitate the activation of locus coeruleus neurons by peripheral stimuli." *Brain Research* 186 (1980): 492–498.

6. Aghajanian, G.K., and Marek, G.J. "Serotonin model of schizophrenia: emerging role of glutamate mechanisms." *Brain Research Reviews* 31 (2000): 302–312.

7. Halpern, John H. and Harrison G. Pope, Jr. "Do hallucinogens residual neuropsychological toxicity?" *Drug and Alcohol Dependence* 53 (1999): 247–256.

8. Cohen, M.M., Hirschhorn, K., and Frosch, W.A. "In vivo and in vitro chromosomal damage induced by LSD-25." *New England Journal of Medicine* 277 (1967): 1043–1049.

9. Irwin, S., and Egozcue, J. "Chromosomal abnormalities in leukocytes from LSD-25 users." *Science* 157 (1967): 313–314.

10. Muneer, R.S. "Effects of LSD on human chromosomes." *Mutation Research* 51 (1978): 403–10.

11. Margolis, S., and Martin, L. "Anophthalmia in an infant of parents using LSD." *Annals of Ophthalmology* 12 (1980): 1378–1381.

12. Blaho, K., Merigian, K., Winbery, S., Geraci, S.A., and Smartt, C. "Clinical pharmacology of lysergic acid diethylamide: case reports and review of the treatment of intoxication." *American Journal of Therapeutics* 4 (1997): 211–221.

13. Klock, J.C., Boerner, U., and Becker, C.E. "Coma, hyperthermia, and bleeding associated with massive LSD overdose, a report of eight cases." *Clinical Toxicology* 8 (1975): 191–203.

Chapter 5

1. Abraham, H.D., Aldridge, and A.M. "Adverse consequences of lysergic acid diethylamide." *Addiction* 88 (1993): 1327–1334.

2. Hurlbut, K.M. "Drug-induced psychoses." *Emergency Medical Clinics of North America* 9 (1991): 31–52.

3. Strassman, R.J. "Adverse reactions to psychedelic drugs: A review of the literature." *Journal of Nervous and Mental Disease* 172 (1984): 577–595.

4. Huxley, Aldous. *The Doors of Perception and Heaven and Hell.* New York: Harper Perennial Modern Classics, 2004.

5. Lerner, A.G., Gelkopf, M., Skladman, I., Oyffe, I., Finkel, B., Sigal, M., and Weizman, A. "Flashback and Hallucinogen Persisting Perception Disorder: clinical aspects and pharmacological treatment approaches." *Israeli Journal of Psychiatry and Related Sciences* 39 (2002): 92–99.

6. Halpern, J.H., and Pope, Harrison G., Jr. "Hallucinogen persisting perception disorder: what do we know after 50 years?" *Drug and Alcohol Dependence* 69 (2003): 109–119.

7. Cooper, H.A. "Hallucinogenic drugs." *The Lancet* 268 (1955): 1078.

8. Barron, S.P., Lowinger, P., and Ebner, E. "A clinical examination of chronic LSD use in the

community." *Comprehensive Psychiatry* 11 (1970): 69–79.

Chapter 6
1. Whalen, John. "The Trip", *LA Weekly*, July 3–9, 1998. Available online. URL: http://www.laweekly.com/news/news/the-trip/6864/. Accessed February 27, 2008.
2. Dyck, E. "Flashback: Psychiatric experimentation with LSD in historical perspective." *Canadian Journal of Psychiatry* 50 (2005): 381–388.
3. Grof, S. *LSD Psychotherapy.* Alameda, Calif.: Hunter House Publishers, 1994.
4. Osmond, H. and Smythies, J.R. "Schizophrenia: a new approach." *Journal of Mental Science* 98 (1952): 309–315.
5. Osmond, H. "On being mad." *Saskatchewan Psychiatric Services Journal* (1952): 4.
6. Smith, C.M. "A new adjunct to the treatment of alcoholism: the hallucinogenic drugs." *Quarterly Journal for Studies on Alcohol* 19 (1958): 406–417.
7. Smith, C.M. "Some reflections on the possible therapeutic effects of hallucinogens with special reference to alcoholism." *Quarterly Journal for Studies on Alcohol* 20 (1959): 293.
8. Mangini, M. "Treatment of alcoholism using psychedelic drugs: a review of the program of research." *Journal of Psychoactive Drugs* 30 (1998): 381–418.
9. Snider, Jerry. "Has psychology failed the acid test? Stanislav Grof." Available online. URL: http://www.lightparty.com/Spirituality/LSD.html. Accessed February 27, 2008.
10. Doblin, R., Beck, J.E., Chapman, K., and Alioto, M. "Dr. Oscar Janiger's pioneering LSD research: a forty-year follow-up." *Bulletin of the Multidisciplinary Association for Psychedelic Studies,* Spring (1999): 7–21.
11. Nichols, C.D., and Sanders-Bush, E. "A single dose of lysergic acid diethylamide influences gene expression patterns within the mammalian brain." *Neuropsychopharmacology* 26 (2002): 634–642.
12. Nichols, C.D., Garcia, E.E., and Sanders-Bush, E. "Dynamic changes in prefrontal cortex gene expression following lysergic acid diethylamide administration." *Molecular Brain Research* 111 (2003): 182–188.

Chapter 7
1. McKenna, Terence. *The Archaic Revival.* New York: HarperCollins, 1992.

Glossary

2C-B—*see* 4-bromo-2,5-dimethoxyphenethylamine

2C-T-7—*see* 2,5-dimethoxypropylthiophenethylamine

2,5-dimethoxy-4-methylamphetamine—DOM, a hallucinogenic substance.

2,5-dimethoxypropylthiophenethylamine—2C-T-7, a hallucinogenic substance.

4-bromo-2,5-dimethoxyphenethylamine—2C-B, a hallucinogenic substance.

5-HT—5-hydroxytryptamine, a neurotransmitter in the brain; also known as serotonin.

5-MeO-DIPT—*see* 5-methoxy-diisopropyltryptamine.

5-MeO-DMT—*see* 5-methoxy-dimethyltryptamine.

5-methoxy-dimethyltryptamine—5-MeO-DMT, a hallucinogenic substance.

5-methoxy-diisopropyltyptamine—5-MeO-DIPT, a hallucinogenic substance.

acid rock—A nickname for music inspired by LSD's effects, aimed at the LSD-taking subculture of the 1960s.

amygdala—The brain structure that controls emotions and learning.

anesthetic—A substance that inhibits sensations, including touch and pain; a numbing agent.

auditory—Having to do with the sense of hearing.

axons—Long, fiber-like parts of neurons that carry electrical signals.

bad trip—A negative experience, often frightening, that can occur after taking a hallucinogenic substance.

basal forebrain—The part of the brain that controls motivation, waking, and emotion.

cerebral cortex—The part of the brain that is responsible for higher cognitive functions such as thinking, planning, decision making, problem solving, etc.

chromosomes—Structures within the nucleus of a cell that contain genetic material called DNA.

cognitive behavioral therapy—A form of behavioral therapy aimed at improving one's thought patterns (i.e., about the use of drugs) and teaching of coping skills (i.e., to help curb drug cravings or avoid situations that provoke the desire to use drugs).

controlled substance—A drug or other chemical that has its possession and use regulated, particularly the Controlled Substances Act.

crash—Negative emotional and physical experiences that occur after the effects of a hallucinogen or other mind-altering substance wear off.

d-lysergic acid—LSD, a potent hallucinogen.

delirium—Disorientation, lack of awareness of one's surroundings, inability to focus or shift one's attention, and memory loss.

delirium tremens—Also known as DTs; a type of hallucination accompanied by shaking of the arms or legs during severe withdrawal from alcohol consumption.

delusions—False beliefs, often impervious to being changed by presentation of facts to the contrary.

depersonalization—The perception that a part of one's body is not of their own, or an out-of-body experience.

dextromethorphan—A common ingredient in cough medicines; can be hallucinogenic at high doses.

dimethyltryptamine—DMT, a hallucinogenic substance.

dissociative anesthestic—An anesthetic agent that produces out-of-body experiences or strong perceptual distortions about one's own body.

DMT—*see* dimethyltryptamine.

DOM—*see* 2,5-dimethoxy-4-methylamphetamine.

DXM—*see* dextromethorphan.

ecstasy—A stimulant and mild hallucinogen that produces intense feeling of love and empathy; also known as methylenedioxymethamphetamine, or MDMA.

entheogens—Mind-altering substances that are used in a religious manner to communicate with the spiritual world.

ergot—A type of fungus that contains hallucinogenic substances.

ergotism—A type of poisoning that results from ingestion of grains or other foods contaminated with ergot.

euphoria—An extreme sense of well-being and pleasure.

exposure therapy—A type of psychological therapy that involves repeatedly exposing a patient to a stimulus that causes an abnormal anxiety response

Glossary

in order to desensitize the patient to ability of the stimulus to provoke anxiety.

flashbacks—Sudden and unexpected reoccurrences of hallucinations or other events experienced while previously under the influence of a hallucinogen.

frontal cortex—The forward part of the brain, involved in thinking, planning, and impulse control.

glutamate—A type of neurotransmitter in the brain.

hallucination—The perception of something by sight, hearing, touch, smell, or taste that is not real.

hallucinogens—Chemical agents that produce hallucinations.

hallucinogen persisting perception disorder—HPPD, a mental disorder characterized by persistent and disturbing intrusions of perceptions experienced while under the influence of a hallucinogen.

hallucinogenic—Having the ability to produce hallucinations.

hippocampus—A brain structure involved in learning and memory.

hyperthermia—An elevated body temperature.

intramuscular—An injection given into a skeletal muscle such as the biceps or triceps.

introspection—Self-examination, self-awareness.

ketamine—A hallucinogenic anesthetic agent.

locus coeruleus—LC, brain region that contains thousands of neurons that produce the chemical noradrenaline (norepinephrine).

lysergic acid diethylamide—LSD, a potent hallucinogen.

magic mushrooms—A type of wild mushroom that can produce hallucinations.

MDMA—Methylenedioxymethamphetamine, also known as ecstasy.

mescaline - A hallucinogenic substance found in the peyote cactus.

monoamine oxidase inhibitor—MAOI, type of drug that inhibits the metabolic breakdown of certain neurotransmitters.

neurons—Nerve cells.

neurotransmitters—Chemical messengers used by nerve cells.

N-methyl-D-aspartate receptor—A type of receptor used by the neurotransmitter glutamate, also known as the NMDA receptor.

noetic—Intellectual or intuitive knowing.

norepinephrine—A neurotransmitter in the brain.

opioid receptors—A class of receptor proteins that bind neurotransmitters such as endorphins, as well as to opium and its derivatives; are classified as mu, delta, or kappa subtypes.

paranoia—A delusional fear that one is being persecuted, plotted against, pursued, or followed, which persists despite the absence of evidence to support it.

PCP—*see* phencyclidine.

peyote—A type of cactus that contains mescaline.

peyotism—A religion followed by many Native Americans in which the hallucinogen mescaline is used in rituals.

phencyclidine—PCP, a hallucinogenic anesthetic agent.

post-traumatic stress disorder—PTSD, a mental disorder characterized by flashbacks and intrusive thoughts or images from a prior traumatic event.

psilocin—The hallucinogenic metabolite of psilocybin.

psilocybin—A hallucinogenic substance found in certain species of mushrooms.

psychedelic—Mind-altering, usually characterized by hallucinations or alterations in sensation and perception.

psychosis—A mental state characterized by a loss of touch with reality, hallucinations, delusions, and disordered thought patterns.

psychotomimetic—A substance that produces a temporary state of psychosis.

raves—Dance parties that feature electronic music and light shows, at which attendees (frequently teenagers and college students) often use hallucinogenic drugs to enhance their experience.

receptors—Specialized proteins localized on the surface of a nerve cell that recognizes a specific neurotransmitter.

salvinorin—A hallucinogenic substance found in the plant *Salvia divinorum*.

Glossary

schedule—The classification of drug substances used by the Drug Enforcement Administration based on the medical usefulness of a particular substance and its potential to cause addiction.

shamanic—Having to do with to shamanism, which is a set of traditional beliefs dealing with communication with the spiritual world, especially in the sense that certain individuals (called shamans, or medicine men) can help heal the ills of a person through communication with spirits.

sensory cortex—The part of the brain that receives and processes information from the senses.

serotonin—A type of neurotransmitter in the brain, also known as 5-hydroxytryptamine.

synapse—The junction between a nerve fiber ending and a neighboring nerve cell.

synaptic terminal—The mushroom-shaped ending of a nerve fiber.

synesthesia—The "crossing over" or blending of two or more senses; e.g., hearing colors or seeing sounds.

tolerance—The phenomenon by which the same dose of a drug has less of an effect after it is taken repeatedly; thought to result from the body's adaptation to the continued presence of the drug.

trip—An individual experience after taking a hallucinogenic substance.

truth drug or truth serum—A substance that potentially would force an unwilling person to communicate the truth.

visual cortex—The part of the brain that receives and processes visual information.

withdrawal—A state of general psychological and physical unpleasantness that occurs following abrupt discontinuation of a drug.

Bibliography

General

Petechuk, David. *LSD* (Drug Education Library). Detroit: Thomson-Gale, 2005.

Chapter 3

Lee, Martin A., and Bruce Shlain. *Acid Dreams – The Complete Social History of LSD: The CIA, the Sixties, and Beyond.* New York: Grove Press, 1992.

Chapter 7

Erowid. Erowid: Documenting the complex relationship between humans and psychoactives. Available online. URL: http://www.erowid.org/chemicals/lsd/. Accessed March 18, 2008.

Further Reading

Black, David. *Acid: A New Secret History of LSD*. London: Vision Paperbacks, 2003.

Hofmann, Albert. *LSD – My Problem Child*. Sarasota, Fla.: Multidisciplinary Association for Psychedelic Studies (MAPS), 2005.

Pletscher, Alfred, and Dieter Ladewig, eds. *Fifty Years of LSD: Current Status and Perspective of Hallucinogens*. Oxford: Taylor and Francis, 1994.

Snow, Otto. *LSD*. Spring Hill, Fla.: Thoth Press, 2003.

Stevens, Jay. *Storming Heaven: LSD the American Dream*. New York: Grove Press, 1998.

Web Sites

Department of Health and Human Services, and Substance Abuse and Mental Health Services Administration. National Clearinghouse for Alcohol and Drug Information
http://ncadi.samhsa.gov

Drug Enforcement Administration
http://www.usdoj.gov/dea/concern/concern.htm

Drug Abuse Resistance Education (D.A.R.E.)
http://www.dare.com

National Institute on Drug Abuse (NIDA)
http://www.drugabuse.gov

NIDA for Teens
http://teens.drugabuse.gov

National Youth Anti-Drug Media Campaign
http://www.theantidrug.com

Office of National Drug Control Policy
http://www.whitehousedrugpolicy.gov

Partnership for a Drug Free America
http://www.drugfree.org

Index

A, 16. *See also* LSD
acid, 16. *See also* LSD
acid rock, 29
acid tests, 29
addiction, 52
Addiction Research Center
(Lexington, KY), 37
Afghanistan War, 59
Alaska, 19
alcohol
addiction to, 13
drug use and, 8
LSD as treatment for,
26, 66
N-methyl-D-aspartate
receptor, 83
religious uses, 6
Alpert, Richard, 30
Alzheimer's disease, 46
Amanita fungi, 6
American Psychiatric
Association, 58
amphetamines, 35
amygdala, 20
anesthetic, 80
angel dust, 82. *See also*
phencyclidine
animal, 16. *See also* LSD
antipsychotic medications,
56
appetite, loss of, as physical
effect of LSD, 43
art, LSD's influence on,
29
auditory cortex, 17
Australia, 19
authority, rebellion against,
28
axons, 15
ayahuasca, 76
Aztecs and drug use, 10

bad trip. *See* trip, bad trip
barbiturates, 35
barrels, 16. *See also* LSD
basal forebrain, 20
battery acid, 16. *See also*
LSD
The Beatles, 29

bees, 78. *See also* 4-
bromo-2,5-dimethoxy-
phenethylamine
Belgium, 19
big D, 16. *See also* LSD
binges, 13
black star, 16. *See also* LSD
blood pressure increase as
physical effect of hal-
lucinogens, 13, 42
blotter acid, 16. *See also*
LSD
blue heaven, 16. *See also*
LSD
blue mist, 16. *See also* LSD
blue moons, 16. *See also*
LSD
Blue Mystic, 78
body temperature increase
as physical effect of hallucinogens, 13, 42
boomers, 16. *See also* LSD
Braden, William, 45
brain
hallucinogens and, 15–17,
49
regions/functions affected
by hallucinogens, 17, 20
toxicity to LSD, 52–53
brain scans, 17, 20
brainstem, 20
Brave New World (Huxley),
26
Brotherhood of Eternal
Love, 30
Buddhism, 28, 47
businessman's trip, 76
The Byrds, 29

California sunshine, 16. *See
also* LSD
candy flipping, 16
Carter, Jimmy, 39
Central Intelligence Agency
(CIA), 34–40
Office of Scientific
Intelligence, 35
cerebellum, 20
cerebral cortex, 49–50

chills as physical effect of
LSD, 42
China, 37, 38
chlorpromazine, 45, 56
Christianity, 10, 28
chromosomes, 53
Church, Frank, 38, 39
Church Committee,
38–39
CIA. *See* Central
Intelligence Agency
civil rights movement, 28
Claviceps purpurea, 21
clozapine, 56
cocaine, 6, 13, 17, 32
Cold War, 38
color, perception of, 12
concentration camps, 35,
37
consciousness, stream of,
46
controlled substance, 19,
32, 86
Controlled Substances Act,
32, 86
Cooper, H. A., 60
Copelandia, 73. *See also*
psilocin
cough medicine, 82
crack, 32
crash, 75
Cuba, 38
cubes, 16. *See also* LSD

Dass, Ram. *See* Alpert,
Richard
DEA. *See* Drug
Enforcement Agency
Delaware, 19,
delirium, 23
delirium tremens (DT), 66
delusions, 14
depersonalization as psy-
chological effect of
LSD, 44, 46, 60
depression, 69
dextromethorphan (DXM),
80–85
diazepam. *See* Valium

Index

Index

Index

About the Author

M. Foster Olive received a bachelor's degree in psychology from the University of California at San Diego and went on to receive a Ph.D. in neuroscience from UCLA. He is currently an assistant professor in the Center for Drug and Alcohol Programs and Department of Psychiatry and Behavioral Sciences at the Medical University of South Carolina. His research focuses on the neurobiology of addiction, and he has published in numerous academic journals, including *Psychopharmacology* and *The Journal of Neuroscience*. He has also authored several books in the Drugs: The Straight Facts Series, including *Peyote and Mescaline, Sleep Aids, Prescription Pain Relievers, Designer Drugs,* and *Crack*.

About the Editor

David J. Triggle is a university professor and a distinguished professor in the School of Pharmacy and Pharmaceutical Sciences at the State University of New York at Buffalo. He studied in the United Kingdom and earned a B.Sc. in chemistry from the University of Southampton and a Ph.D. in chemistry at the University of Hull. Following postdoctoral work at the University of Ottawa in Canada and the University of London in the United Kingdom, he assumed a position at the School of Pharmacy at Buffalo. He served as chairman of the Department of Biochemical Pharmacology from 1971 to 1985, and as dean of the School of Pharmacy from 1985 to 1995. From 1995 to 2001, he served as the dean of the graduate school and as the university provost from 2000 to 2001. He is the author of several books dealing with the chemical pharmacology of the autonomic nervous system and drug-receptor interactions, some 400 scientific publications, and he has delivered more than 1,000 lectures worldwide on his research.